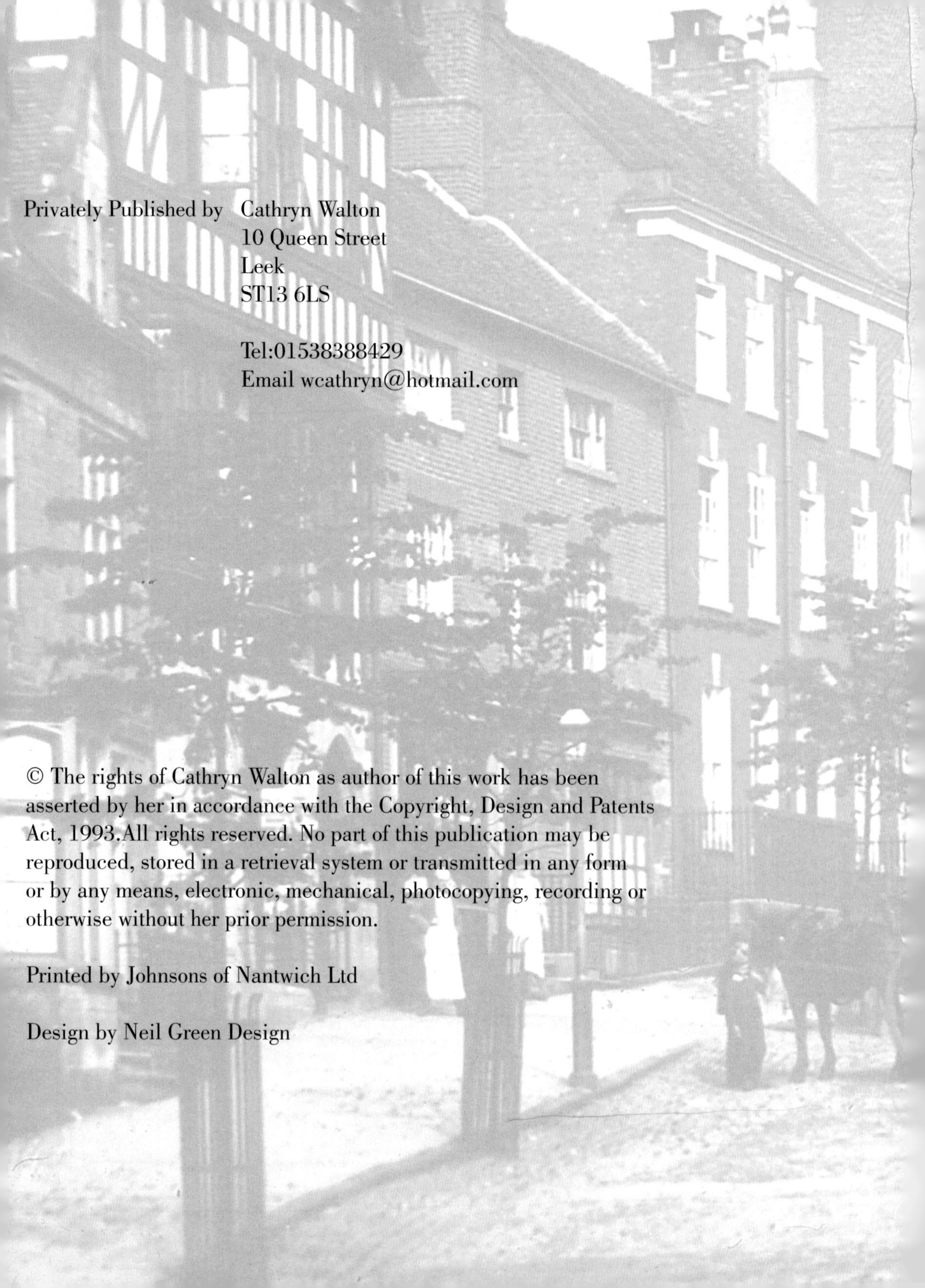

Privately Published by Cathryn Walton
10 Queen Street
Leek
ST13 6LS

Tel:01538388429
Email wcathryn@hotmail.com

Printed by Johnsons of Nantwich Ltd

Design by Neil Green Design

HIDDEN LIVES

Leek's Extraordinary Embroiderers

Cathryn Walton

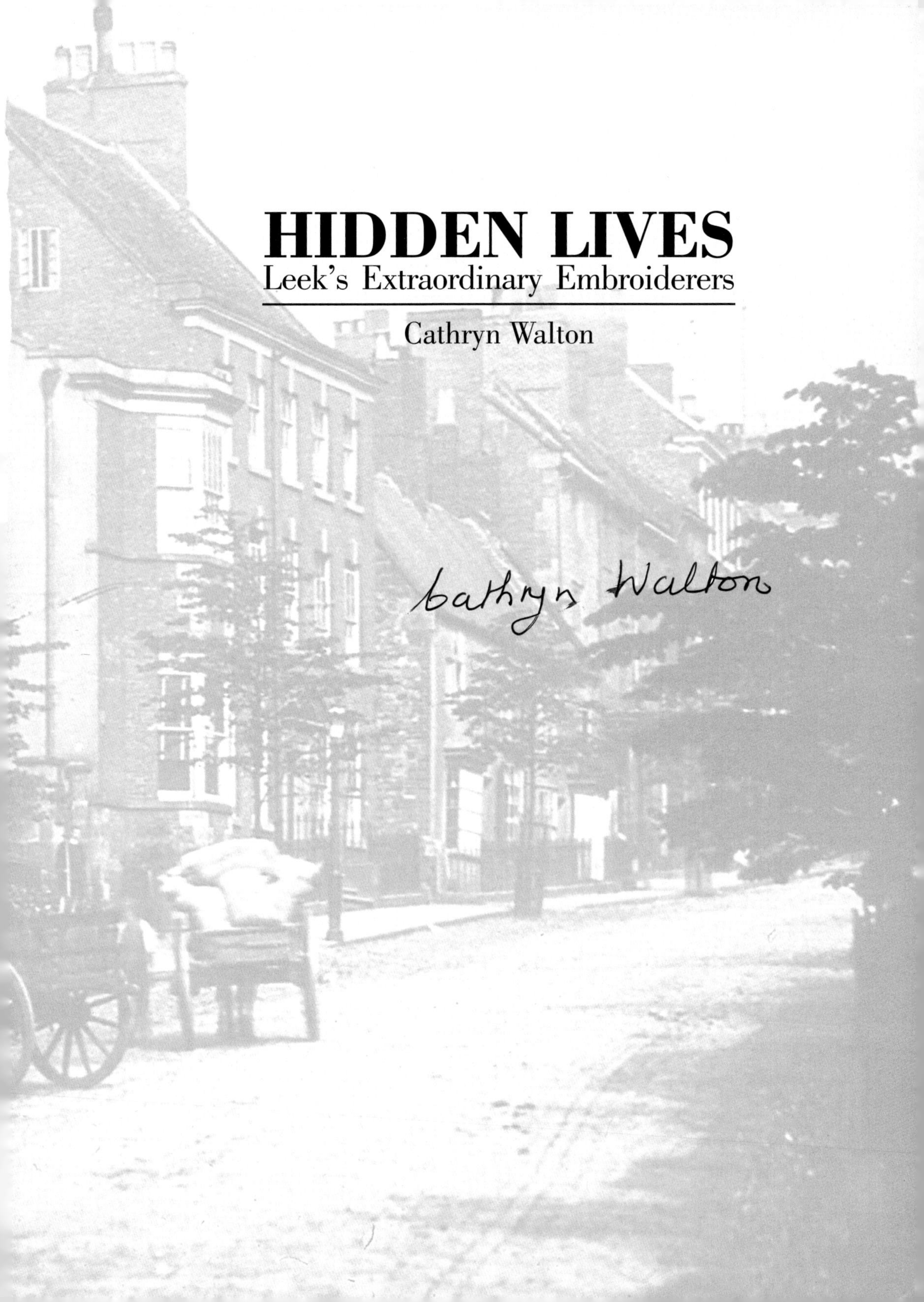

Cathryn Walton

Contents

Introduction

Many exquisite embroideries, stitched by the Leek Embroidery Society, still survive. They remain a testament to the skill and artistry of the women who stitched them. Although the embroideries themselves have been described in several publications little is known about the women who stitched them. This book hopes to bring the women out of the wings and place them centre stage where they belong.

Right
Elizabeth Wardle (centre) with some of her pupils

As no archive has survived relating to the Leek Embroidery Society it is impossible to discover the names of all the women who contributed to the work of the society. It is well known that the Leek Embroidery Society existed from 1879 to circa. 1930 and that Elizabeth Wardle was its superintendent until her death in 1902, but the organization of the society and of the women who were members is not known. We don't know how one became a member of the society, although two legal contracts drawn up between Elizabeth Wardle and women who were about to work for her have been discovered. These confirm that some women were paid and had to adhere to strict instructions regarding their hours of work and conditions of employment. However, it is doubtful that wives and daughters of wealthy silk manufacturers, solicitors and professional men, who are also described as members of the Society, would be paid for their work. These women often helped to embroider ecclesiastical pieces including altar and super frontals, litany and pulpit falls for churches at home and abroad. Most of the women were members of the congregations at local churches; they helped to decorate the churches during Harvest Festivals and provided refreshments and entertainment at church socials. As young women many of them attended Art Classes at the Mechanics Institute in Russell Street. They stitched items for their own homes including fire screens, cushion covers, table runners, decorative borders for curtains and mantels, chair guards, tea cozies and nightdress cases.

Leek was a relatively small market town where social opportunities were limited so that women who did not work shared the same activities. They took part in amateur dramatics, sang or played instruments at concerts, attended performances by the Leek Amateur Musical Society, the Philothespian Club and Leek Amateur Opera Society. They danced at balls held at the Red Lion, the Swan and the Town Hall. Several of the women were members of the Leek branch of the Primrose League (Cruso habitation) and served on various committees including that of the Leek Charity Organization Society.

Additionally these women moved in the same social circle, many of them were related to Thomas and Elizabeth Wardle or to each other.

The young women who worked for Elizabeth Wardle at the Embroidery Society premises at 56 St Edward Street were mostly the daughters of tradesmen. Their families, more often that not, lived within walking distance of St Edward Street and Thomas Wardle most probably did business with their fathers. These women included the daughter of the blacksmith, whose smithy stood at the top of St Edward Street and the daughters of the wine merchant whose premises were just around the corner. Ann Cartwright's father was an ironmonger in a street off the Market Place and both Sarah Price and Charlotte Robinson were daughters of men who worked for the Challinor family, who were Thomas Wardle's solicitors. Interestingly, Mary Ann Bishop, whose father was Thomas Wardle's cousin, was the only girl who had been working in the silk mills before being employed by Elizabeth Wardle.

The names of the women who were paid employees of the Embroidery Society have been gleaned from a photograph, dated 1888, names attached to the 'Four Kings' frontal in St Edward's church in Leek, family memories and by occupations on various census returns. No doubt there are other women who worked for the Leek Embroidery Society who have yet to be discovered.

The Pelican Frontal

Although the Leek Embroidery Society was established in 1879, Elizabeth Wardle and a group of women had been perfecting their skills for some years when stitching ecclesiastical embroideries. In 1872 Elizabeth and ten other women were busily engaged in embroidering an altar cloth for St. Luke's Church in Leek. An entry in *St Luke's Church Magazine* dated September 1872 refers to the band of ladies who were busily engaged in embroidering the 'Pelican Altar Frontal', which would replace one that had been in use since the church was consecrated in 1848. The members of the congregation had contributed varying sums towards the cost of a new super frontal and had raised nearly £10. However, as the cost of this super frontal was estimated to be £25 other donations were needed. If this is correct this super frontal, which cannot be traced, would have cost well over £1,000 today. It is possible that the magazine may be referring to the cost of the Pelican Frontal and not the super frontal.

Background Image
Detail form the Pelican Frontal

holy

Above
Pelican Frontal

The beautiful Pelican Frontal, designed by John D Sedding and embroidered by Elizabeth Wardle and ten other women, was presented to the church in 1873. It can still be seen in St Luke's Church and is obviously the work of skilled needlewomen. At least two of the women who embroidered it went on to stitch for the Leek Embroidery Society. A tape stitched to the top of the frontal records the names of the needlewomen. Most of them were members of St Luke's congregation. Their stories are told in this chapter.

Right
St Luke's Church
with Pelican Frontal
on the altar

Ann Clowes
1830-1897

Ann Clowes was a woman of independent means who lived in the prestigious Park Villas in Park Road, Leek. The house was one of two semi-detached villas built on land which was formerly part of the Ball Haye estate. The house later became known as 'Beechfields' and the villa next door as 'The Park'. Ann's neighbour was John Brough, a silk manufacturer, who with his brother, Joseph, had purchased Ball Haye Hall and 42 acres of land in 1853.

Ann Clowes was a spinster who lived with her mother, until she died, and then by herself with a cook and a housemaid. No occupation is recorded for Ann on the census returns dated 1861; however subsequent census returns record Ann as an annuitant or as 'living on her own means'.

Ann's income came from the Badnall dye-works which were situated by the River Churnet on the corner of Mill Street and Abbey Green Road. Ann Badnall, who had inherited the Badnall family dye-works, left the use of the dye-house premises to members of the Clowes family for life in her will. Ann Clowes was able to gain income from them for the rest of her life. John Clowes, Ann's father, had worked for Ann Badnall as her foreman dyer. The dye-houses were rented by the Hammersley family and the premises in Leek are always spoken of as 'Hammersley's Dye-works'.

As Ann Clowes was only 6 years old when she inherited the use of the dye-works, it would be her mother, confusingly also named Ann, who acted for her daughter. Ann Clowes senior died at Park Villas in 1861 leaving her daughter goods and chattels valued at under £5,000.

Ann Clowes knew the Wardle family as her dye-works were situated close to the Hencroft and Churnet Work dye-works operated by Thomas Wardle. They had a shared interest in maintaining the water supply from the River Churnet to their respective dye-works. In 1870, Ann Clowes had complained that a reservoir built by the Staffordshire Potteries Waterworks Company had led to the muddying of the waters of the River

Above
Park Villas, Ann's home was on the left

Churnet near to her dye-works. Both Ann and her tenant William Hammersley emphasized the importance of the silk trade to Leek saying that pure water was essential for washing and dyeing silk. Planks were thrown across the River Churnet on which the workers stood to lower hanks of silk into the waters to remove excess dye.

The income from the dye-works and other investments enabled Ann to lead a comfortable life; she owned a substantial house with a large garden and was able to employ servants. Park Villas were just a short distance from Ball Haye Hall once the home of the Worthington sisters and quite close to St Luke's vicarage where Elizabeth Pidcock lived. Ann Clowes, Rose and Alice Worthington and Elizabeth Pidcock were neighbours who worshipped at St Luke's Church where Benjamin Pidcock was the vicar. These near neighbours all helped to stitch the Pelican Frontal for St Luke's in 1873. St Luke's Parish Registers reveal that Miss Ann Clowes made generous contributions to church funds over many years. Ann also embroidered a pulpit fall for the church and stitched panel 4 of the facsimile of the Bayeux Tapestry.

Above
Hammersley's dye-works can be seen on the right. The tall chimney in the centre of the photograph shows the location of the Hencroft works

A document dated 1859 reveals that Ann Clowes had demised the dye-works by indenture dated 13 November 1859 to William Henry Hammersley and his assigns for one year and thereafter from year to year renewable until notice to quit was given by either side. The yearly rent was £120 with Hammersley paying all taxes except the landlord's property tax and doing all repairs to the premises.

Sarah Needham

No information has been discovered about the identity of Sarah Needham who was one of the embroiderers of the Pelican Frontal. Apart from Elizabeth Pidcock, who was the vicar's wife, all of the women who stitched this frontal did not have occupations and for the most part had independent incomes. A Sarah Needham is recorded on the 1871 census return, who might be the elusive embroiderer. She was born in Leek in 1846 and is described as a gentlewoman and a proprietor of houses on the census return. She is lodging at the house of Charles Henry Carlisle in Hollinsclough, a village not far from Leek, in the Peak District. Charles Henry Carlisle was the vicar of Quarnford at this time.
Could this be the elusive needlewoman?

Elizabeth Pidcock (nee Smith)
1847-1911

Below, right
St Luke's Church

Below, top left
St Luke's Vicarage

Below, bottom left
St Mary's Church in Easton where Lucy Pidcock married Arthur Wardle

Elizabeth Smith was born in Manchester and married Benjamin Pidcock in 1866 at St Paul's Church in Chorlton on Medlock. Benjamin Pidcock was almost thirty years older than Elizabeth and was the vicar at St Luke's Church in Fountain Street in Leek, a post he had held from the consecration of the church in 1848. Elizabeth was the daughter of Charles and Mary Smith and although she was born in Manchester her family did have connections with Leek. Her father had been a draper in Custard Street (now Stanley Street) and her mother was the daughter of Richard Etches, who had been a wine merchant in the town.

Above
Benjamin Pidcock,
Elizabeth's husband

Elizabeth lived in St Luke's vicarage which had been built in the 1850s on land formerly part of the Ball Haye Hall estate; today it is home to a veterinary practice. One of Elizabeth's near neighbours was Ann Clowes, who also stitched for the embroidery society. It is hardly surprising that Elizabeth Pidcock was one of the early embroiderers, supervised by Elizabeth Wardle, who helped to stitch the Pelican Frontal for her husband's church in 1873. Elizabeth also stitched part of the Khartoum Frontal in 1905 and records show that she stitched a Jacobean design fire screen in pinks and greens. Reports in local newspapers show that Elizabeth Pidcock supported her husband's work in his Leek parish hosting tea parties, organizing bazaars, singing at concerts and helping at other parish functions.

Benjamin and Elizabeth had nine children, their daughter, Lucy, married Arthur Henry Wardle in 1898. Arthur was one of the sons of Thomas and Elizabeth Wardle and became a partner in the firm of silk dyers, well known in Leek as Sir T & A Wardle & Co. They were married in St Mary's Church in Easton in Hampshire where Benjamin Pidcock was the rector. The Pidcock family had left Leek in 1883 and lived in Easton for seventeen years.

After Benjamin's death Elizabeth returned to Leek living at 1 Shirburn Terrace in Ashbourne Road, where she died in 1911. Her daughters continued to live there after her death.

Fanny Shute
1846 - 1929

Frances Amelia Shute, the daughter of Frederick Gay Shute and his wife Amelia, was born in 1847 in Friday Street, London. Her father was born in Gosport and worked as a land and estate agent plying his trade in London, Millbrook and Winchester before moving to Leek. The Shute family was only in Leek for a relatively short period of time. In 1871 they lived in Leek at Regent House, 31 Regent Street. Fanny's father's business premises were situated at 1, Church Lane in Leek. While living in Regent Street, Fanny helped to stitch the Pelican Frontal for St Luke's Church. Regent Street is near to St Luke's where the Shute family worshipped. Fanny and her sisters helped with entertainments and tea parties in aid of the church while they lived there.

The Shute family moved to Derby after 1873 but Fanny's brother Charles Edward, a commercial traveller in silk, married a Leek girl and remained in the town.

Fanny never married and lived with her parents at 11 Arboretum Square in Derby until they died and after their deaths lived at 14 Norfolk Street in Derby with her niece. Fanny Shute had an income from 'private means' which supported her in Derby until her death in 1929.

Right
Regent House in
Leek

Right
Arboretum Square
in Derby

The Sutton Sisters

Mary Ellen Sutton
1838 -1892

Ann Bateman Sutton
1841-1891

Mary Ellen and Ann were born in Huddersfield, the daughters of William and Mary Sutton. William Sutton was a coal merchant in Huddersfield who died there in 1846. The girls remained with their mother in Huddersfield for some years but had moved to Leek by 1861 when they lived with her in Fountain Place. Both their parents had been born in Leek, William Sutton's father kept the grocers shop on the corner of Leek Market Place and Sheep Market while Mary's father, Joseph Lowndes, was the innkeeper at the 'Roebuck' in Derby Street. After their mother's death the sisters moved from Fountain Place to live with their aunt on Clerk Bank. She was their mother's sister and the widow of Josiah Brunt, a Leek silk manufacturer.

Benjamin Pidcock, the vicar at St Luke's Church, married Mary Ellen Sutton to Levi Ellerton in 1875, just two years after she and her sister had helped to stitch the Pelican Frontal for the church. Mary Ellen was Levi Ellerton's second wife and helped him to run his drapers shop in Derby Street in Leek. Levi and Mary Ellen lived at 39 Queen Street, an imposing detached house, which later became the home of a Leek silk manufacturer and which is now the premises of an undertaker. Mary Ellen, who never had children, was a relatively wealthy woman when she died leaving an estate of £2,829.

Ann Bateman Sutton was married in 1875 to Matthew Turbitt at Christ Church in Southport but lived in Fountain Place in Leek in 1881. Ann died in Southport in 1890 but her husband lived on until 1928. Matthew describes himself as a gentleman and had sufficient funds to enable him to set up a scholarship for the education and training of young people in the Sefton area.

Above
39 Queen Street now named Lyndhurst House, the home of Levi Ellerton and his wife Mary Ellen (nee Sutton)

Elizabeth Wardle
1834-1902

Elizabeth Wardle's name is placed at the centre of the list of names stitched on a tape at the top of the Pelican Frontal.
She is featured in 'The Wardle Family' chapter.

Catherine Whittles
1847 -1928

Catherine was the daughter of John and Lucy Whittles, who kept the grocer's shop at 16 Market Place in Leek. She is a relative of the Sutton sisters whose grandfather had the grocers shop there in previous years. The premises fronted on to the Market Place but also stretched round the corner into Sheep Market.
Catherine Whittle was educated at a school in St John Street in Ashbourne which was run by a schoolmistress and five governesses. Catherine was one of twenty five young women who were educated there. Her father died when she was eighteen, so she helped her mother in the shop. Catherine was in her forties and still a spinster when her mother died in 1891 and appears to have spent the rest of her life living with relatives.
Interestingly her uncle, Thomas Whittles, started a silk business which became Thomas Whittles & Co. Ltd. This was located at the Wellington Mill in Strangman Street in Leek. Descendants of the Whittle family continued to operate from Wellington Mill until 1994. At that time they were providing silk buttonhole twist for tailors in Savile Row in London.

Above
Whittles & Son's premises in Sheep Market

The Worthington Sisters

Alice Worthington
1844-1916

Rose Worthington
1847 -1926

Rose and Alice Worthington were daughters of Andrew Jukes Worthington, a Leek silk manufacturer, and his wife Sarah. Andrew was the founder of AJ Worthington & Co whose silk mills stood in Queen Street and Portland Street in Leek. They manufactured sewing threads, bindings, braids and trimmings. Andrew had a workforce of 200 employees at his mills in 1861. The Worthington's had lived at Horton Hall, a few miles from Leek, before moving to 47 St Edward Street in Leek, where both Alice and Rose were born. Here the Worthington children were cared for by a nurse and an under nurse. A cook prepared the family meals and a domestic servant looked after the housework. This house, now a dentist's surgery, was just across the road from Thomas and Elizabeth Wardle's home. Obviously the two families were connected by their respective roles in the silk industry and as neighbours would have socialized together. Indeed, in 1889 Philip Jukes Worthington, the younger brother of Rose and Alice, married Margaret Elizabeth Wardle, one of the daughters of Thomas and Elizabeth Wardle. Rose and Alice led privileged lives as befitting their status as daughters of a wealthy silk manufacturer. They attended the 1867 Annual Ball in the assembly rooms at the Red Lion with their parents. The Worthingtons moved to Ball Haye Hall in 1870, a spacious mansion with dining and drawing rooms, breakfast room and study as well as rooms for the butler, housekeeper and servants. Ten bedrooms, four dressing rooms and hot and cold baths were located on the first floor with accommodation for servants above. The extensive grounds included a lake and island, a plantation and 26 acres of parkland. Although the hall has been demolished a portion of the grounds are

Below
On the left of this photograph is 47 St Edward Street where the Worthington sisters were born

Right
Print of Ball Haye Hall

Right
Portland Mill today

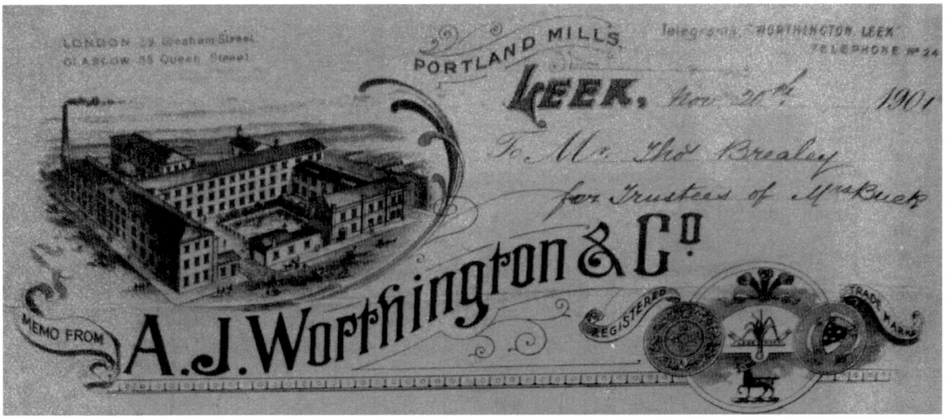

Above
AJ Worthington & Co. Letterhead

now part of Leek's Brough Park where Leek families can wander through the gardens, play tennis or watch their children happily feeding the ducks on the lake. Ball Haye Hall was situated near to the current Park Road and just below Leek's present public swimming baths. At Ball Haye the Worthington's nearest neighbours were two members of the Leek Embroidery Society, Ann Clowes at Park Villas and Elizabeth Pidcock at St Luke's Vicarage. Benjamin Pidcock was the vicar at St Luke's where the Worthington family worshipped and where Andrew Worthington had served as a churchwarden. The Worthington children donated the choir stalls in St Luke's Church in memory of their father: the carved angels were added to the stalls a little later in memory of Andrew's son, Ernest Worthington. Memorial plaques dedicated to Andrew Worthington and his sons can be seen in the church.

Right
Regent House in Regent Street, former home of Alice Worthington

After her parents died, Alice Worthington lived with her brother, Philip, at Regent House in Regent Street, Leek. After Philip married she continued to live there, employing a cook and a housekeeper. For many years Alice served on the committee of the Leek Charity Organization Society and remained a faithful and supportive member of St Luke's congregation all her life. In 1900 she opened a sale of work at St Luke's when the vicar remarked that her family had taken a helpful interest in the church from its beginning. Alice was a spinster and died in Regent Street in 1916. Interestingly, Regent House, which became Alice's home, was previously lived in by the Shute family before they moved to Derby. Many houses in Leek were rented and had several different tenants over the years.

Above
Reverend Augustus Wirgman, Husband of Rose Worthington

Rose Worthington had a very different life as she married the Reverend Augustus Wirgman in January 1874 at St. Luke's Church. Augustus, son of the Vicar of Hartington, had recently been appointed as the Vice Principal of St Andrew's College in Grahamstown in South Africa. A few days after their wedding the couple sailed from Dartmouth to Cape Town on the 'Edinburgh Castle' a ship of the famous Castle Line of mail steamers. The voyage took about twenty four days taking Rose to a very different life than that she had known in Leek.

Augustus Wirgman became the rector at St Mary's Church in Port Elizabeth in 1875 and later became rural dean there. The Wirgmans returned to England in 1882 for a six month holiday as Augustus was concerned about his wife's health and felt that they both needed a break. According to Augustus Wirgman in *'Storm and Sunshine'* Rose's health was "wonderfully improved" after her time in England.
In 1893 the Wirgman's felt in need of "rest and change" so they returned to England again, this time on the U.S.S Pretoria. They were appreciative of "the fresh beauties of an English spring after the heat and dust of South Africa". While staying in London Augustus had a meeting with Frederick Temple, who was at that time the Bishop of London. He invited Rose and her husband to a garden party at Fulham Palace which was then the main residence of the Bishops of London.

The Leek Embroidery Society made a set of Altar frontals for the church in Port Elizabeth after it was destroyed by arson in 1895. Naturally Rose, who kept in touch with her friends and family in Leek, would enlist the help of skilled needlewomen in her home town. Unfortunately the same arsonist struck again just two years later, destroying the altar, resulting in a request to the Leek Embroidery Society to supply a new altar and super frontal in violet.

Right
The Rose Wirgman Memorial Gateway, St Mary's Collegiate Church, Port Elizabeth

Rose would have experienced great changes in Port Elizabeth as during the Boer War thousands of soldiers, horses and materials, landed there before heading to the front by railway. Although the city was not involved in any conflict many refugees moved there, including Boer women and children, who were interred in British concentration camps.
In 1900 Rose wrote in a letter home that

> *"times are very bad in South Africa just now provisions are dear and money is scarce, still I think Port Elizabeth people are very good, we do the best we can for our own refugees and don't forget our "soldiers' comforts". My husband is as busy as he can be as he is Military Chaplain to the troops in Port Elizabeth and has charge of the lines of communication between here and Naauwport."*

After the war ended Rose and her husband went back to England for a period of rest. Augustus wrote that he needed it badly after having had the full responsibility of his parochial work as well as his military duties. They sailed on the troop steamer 'Plassey' where Augustus served as the ship's chaplain to the eight hundred troops on board. After spending some time in England the Wirgmans travelled to the continent visiting Milan, Florence, Pisa and Rome. In 1911, Rose Wirgman is staying with her sister Emily Goodman in Lichfield while Augustus is in a hotel in London. Augustus died in Africa in 1917 and Rose in Stoke-on-Trent in 1926. The Rose Wirgman Memorial Gateway was erected at St Mary's Collegiate Church in Port Elizabeth in her memory.

Mary Young
1850-1921

Mary was the daughter of Samuel and Catherine Young who farmed at Lyme House in Longsdon and was Elizabeth Wardle's cousin. Elizabeth Wardle's mother, also Elizabeth (nee Young), had lived at Lyme House with her brother and his family in the 1870s.

Mary Young was living with her father and sisters at Lyme House when she helped to stitch the Pelican frontal, but moved to Gratton in 1879 after her marriage to Thomas Hulme at St Luke's Church in Endon. Thomas and Mary Hulme farmed 142 acres at Gratton Hall where they employed seven farm labourers. Later they moved to Endon Bank where Thomas worked as a land agent and clay merchant before starting up a ceramic transfer business in Newcastle-under-Lyme.

According to Robert Ferguson in his book *'The Short Sharp Life of T.E.Hulme'*, Mary Hulme (nee Young) was described by her daughter as a spirited independent woman with a good sense of humour and a command of repartee. She was a keen cyclist who took her bicycle abroad with her on several occasions. She would have been very proud of her son Thomas Ernest Hulme who, before he died in battle on Flanders fields, became a modernist poet and critic and played an important role in early 20th century literary and cultural history. There is a memorial window to Thomas E Hulme in St Luke's Church at Endon.

Right
Lyme House, the home of Mary Young

Right
Endon Bank where Mary Young lived after her marriage

The Facsimile of the Bayeux Tapestry

In 1885 Sir Philip Cunliffe-Owen from South Kensington Museum showed Thomas and Elizabeth Wardle a set of hand coloured cartoons of the Bayeux Tapestry. The tapestry is in fact an embroidery and was stitched using coloured wools on bleached linen. It fascinated and interested Elizabeth so much that she decided that 'England should have a copy of its own'. After the Wardle's had visited France to study the original tapestry Thomas Wardle began the work of dying worsted wool to match the faded shades in the tapestry. Vegetable dyes were used, at the Churnet Works, and in all 100lbs of worsted wool was dyed using madder, woad, walnut roots and weld. Cartoons of the tapestry were borrowed from South Kensington and traced by Lizzie Allen.

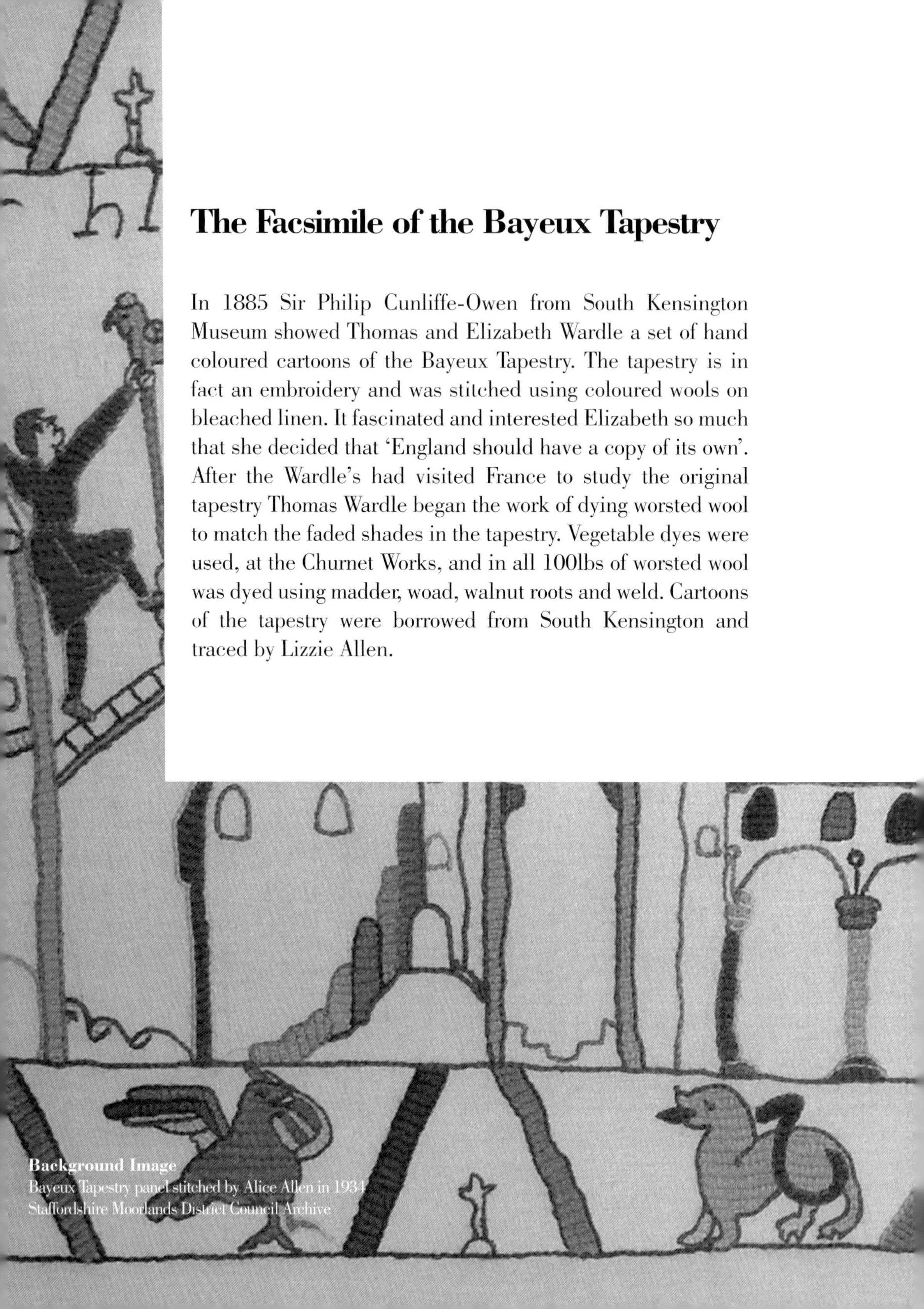

Background Image
Bayeux Tapestry panel stitched by Alice Allen in 1934
Staffordshire Moorlands District Council Archive

PVS:EADWARDI:REG

Above
Illustrated guide to the Facsimile of the Bayeux Tapestry when it was exhibited at Port Elizabeth, South Africa in 1931

The 35 women who stitched the tapestry were mostly wives and daughters of silk manufacturers, solicitors and doctors. However, some of Elizabeth Wardle's embroidery pupils and employees from the Leek Embroidery Society also worked on the tapestry. Each woman's contribution varied in length and each stitched their signatures on the panel that they had worked. Additionally two women pressed the panels before they were joined and another stitched the individual panels together.

The 230 foot long embroidery was finished by June 1886 and displayed in the Nicholson Institute where the public paid 1/- per head to see it. It was later exhibited in many parts of the country before going to America, Europe and South Africa.

To Elizabeth Wardle's disappointment this important work was sold to Reading in 1895 and is now on display in Reading Museum. The women in this chapter are those whose only contribution to the work of the Leek Embroidery Society was their needlework on the facsimile of the Bayeux Tapestry. This major project which was completed in one year needed the input of these additional needlewomen. The women who stitched other embroideries as well as the facsimile are included in different chapters.

When the facsimile was sold in 1895 each needlewoman, who had stitched any part of it, received a proportional share of the sale price.

Sarah Iliffe (Edgbaston) and Elizabeth Frost (Taylor) also stitched part of the facsimile of the Bayeux Tapestry. To date is has not been possible to positively identify these women.

Emily Anne Bate (nee Robinson)
1846 – 1921

Emily Anne Bate lived in Derby when she stitched panel 12 of the facsimile of the Bayeux Tapestry. She was married to James Overs Bate who was twenty six years older than her and a colliery manager. Emily Anne was the only daughter of Henry and Elizabeth Robinson; her father was a solicitor and gentleman. Emily was born at the rectory in Whittington in Derbyshire where her grandfather, Robert Robinson, had been the curate of St Bartholomew's church for over fifty years. When Emily married James Overs Bate at Whittington, in 1870, her marriage was announced in several newspapers including the *Sheffield Independent* and the *London Standard*. At the time of their marriage James lived at the Manor House in Whittington where the couple set up home. Later they moved to Derby where all their children were born. In 1882, Mr. and Mrs. James Overs Bate were patrons of a fund raising bazaar held in the Royal Drill Hall in Derby. The bazaar was held to raise money for the building of a school for boys in the parish of St Luke in Derby; Emily was one of the stallholders.

Emily's brother, Robert Henry Robinson, was a mining engineer and surveyor who took out a patent on 'Improvements in Valve Gear for Steam Engines' in 1881. He had worked with Francis Calvert Gillett, another mining engineer, who lived in Duffield. Francis Gillett's daughter, Mary, also stitched a panel of the facsimile of the Bayeux Tapestry. It would seem that the Bate and Gillett families were known to each other but does not explain why they stitched for the Leek Embroidery Society or how they knew of its existence. Although they could have worked on their respective panels at home they would have had to travel to Leek to ensure that there work was compatible with that of other embroiderers. This may be explained by the presence in Derby of Valentine Lunn who also stitched a panel of the tapestry. She is known to have taught at the Leek School of Embroidery and would have been able to supervise the women working on the facsimile who lived in the Derby area.

Emma Jane Bentley
1855-1909

Emma Jane was the daughter of Joseph and Margaret Bentley. Her father was a silk manufacturer who, in 1861, employed 160 hands at his silk mill in Leek. Joseph Bentley had been in partnership with Thomas Whittles at the Wellington silk mill in Strangman Street. This imposing property still stands and now provides sheltered housing for older people.
Unfortunately, in consequence of losses as the result of bad debts and the high price of raw silks, the partners issued a statement of their affairs to their creditors in 1865. One of those creditors was Thomas Wardle who at that time was a silk dyer at Leekbrook.

Below
Southbank Street. Emma lived with her aunt in the terrace on the left

LEEK HIGH SCHOOL

FOR BOYS AND GIRLS.

Governing Body:

THE LEEK MUNICIPAL EDUCATION COMMITTEE.

Chairman:—JOHN HALL, Esq., J.P.

Headmaster:—Mr. T. C. WARRINGTON, M.A., F.C.S.
(Late Scholar of Jesus College, Oxford).

Head Mistress:—Miss MARY BURN, M.A.
(Late Scholar of University College, Liverpool).

Assistant Master:—Mr. J. J. SYKES, Inter. B. A., Lond.

Ditto:—Mr. H. G. MARTYN, A.R.C.S.

Assistant Mistress:—Miss E. M. BARTHOLOMEW, B.A.

Kindergarten Mistress:—Miss ADA TYERS.

Assistant:—Miss JESSIE SUMERLING.

Cookery and Laundry Mistress:—Miss M. SANT.

Music Mistress:—Miss E. J. BENTLEY.

Woodwork Instructor:—Mr. G. B. ORMISTON.

The School will open on Tuesday, September 16, 1902.

Above
Leek High School advert with Emma Jane Bentley listed as Music Mistress

Above, right
The Queen Street Off Licence in later years

Right
10 Queen Street on the right where Emma Jane Bentley lived with her mother in 1881

Joseph Bentley's finances must have suffered as after he died, in 1868, his widow and children had to leave their pleasant house in Fountain Street to live with Ann Jackson. Ann was Margaret Bentley's sister who had an off license shop on the corner of Queen Street and Portland Street.

Emma Jane, at the age of sixteen, was working as a governess and her ten year old brother, Thomas Jackson Bentley, was a pupil at a 'commercial travellers school for orphan and necessitous children' in Pinner at this time. All of which points to the family having little money. By 1881 Emma was a principal of a ladies school and lived with her mother in a town house at the bottom of Queen Street. Coincidentally this is the house which is now the home of the author.

Emma Jane attended lessons at Leek Art Classes where she gained certificates in geometry and both freehand and perspective drawing. She was a talented musician and a Licentiate of the Royal Academy of Music. Emma was the accompanist for Leek Amateur Musical Society for many years and often played the piano at promenade concerts, operettas and other dramatic and musical recitals. She taught at the School of Music at the Art and Technical School in the Nicholson Institute for several years teaching harmony, rudiments of music, pianoforte and clavicle.

In contrast to her brothers, who moved to Leicestershire and Birmingham, Emma Jane lived in Leek all her life. After her mother died, in 1884, she lived with her aunt, Ann Jackson, her mother's sister, at 19 Southbank Street. Emma Jane died in the McAlpine Nursing Home in Glasgow in 1909, she is buried in St Edward's churchyard in Leek.

Elizabeth Eaton (later Mills)
1852-1915

Elizabeth, the daughter of Charles and Jane Eaton, was born at Sutton on the Hill in Derbyshire where her father farmed 250 acres. Her father, a prosperous farmer, employed a housemaid, a dairy maid, a cowman and a carter, no doubt Elizabeth and her siblings would have been expected to help out on the farm too. By 1881 the Eaton family had moved to a smaller farm at The Limes in Etwall and Elizabeth was living there when she helped to stitch the facsimile of the Bayeux Tapestry which was completed in 1886. Just two years later she married Henry Mills, a local solicitor, and set up house with him at 'The Hollies' in Etwall. Sadly Henry died in 1890 leaving Elizabeth with independent means. However her financial situation must have deteriorated as by 1901 she is working as a sick nurse, an occupation she followed until her death.

Right
The Limes in Etwall

Right
St Helen's Church,
Etwall

Patience Elizabeth Gater
1865-1912

Patience, the daughter of Edmond and Sarah Gater, was born in Wetley Rocks, a village near Leek. Her eldest sister, Mary, was also born there but other children were born in Burslem where her father worked in the pottery industry. The Gater family had moved back to Wetley Rocks by the time Patience was born and in 1881 were living at Cornhill Cross in Leek when both Patience and her mother worked as embroiderers. Patience was one of the women who had 'stitched studies in Indian colourings', under the supervision of Elizabeth Wardle, which were displayed in an Art Exhibition at the Temperance Hall in Union Street in 1880. She also worked panel 5 of the replica of the Bayeux Tapestry together with three other girls who worked for Elizabeth Wardle. Family descendants are aware that Patience worked for the Leek Embroidery Society and are adamant that she stitched embroidery for Queen Victoria. Patience married Vernon Poole in 1889; their first home was at 10 Rosebank Street in Leek. Vernon Poole was a Leek man who worked as a silk warehouseman. Patience went into business in her own right and is listed in *Kelly's Directory*, in 1896, as the proprietor of a draper's shop in Haywood Street in Leek. However a letter, dated 1896, reveals she had a shop in Stanley Street. The letter, written by Patience to a Miss Chambre, acknowledges "*receipt of money on security of the goods in her shop in Stanley Street*". Patience must have been experiencing financial difficulties as another letter, written in 1897, refers to the hope that she may be able to pay Miss Chambre something on account each month after January 1898. A letter from Edward Challinor, a Leek solicitor, to Miss Chambre advises her not to destroy Patience's letter. Unfortunately Patience's financial troubles did not improve as a stamped, printed official notice to a creditor was issued in Staffordshire County Court under the Bankruptcy Act in April 1899 to Mary Chambre of Kensington, London under an administration order against Vernon and Patience Poole of Leek. When she resided in Leek Miss Chambre lived at 30

St Edward Street which she rented from the Turnock family whose daughter Mary Elizabeth was also a member of the Leek Embroidery Society.
By 1901 Vernon and Patience are living apart, he has returned to his parents' home in Leek while Patience is working as a seamstress in Chorlton. Perhaps their straitened circumstances were responsible for this temporary arrangement as in 1911 both Patience and her husband are living in Oldham. Patience is still working as a seamstress there and Vernon as an iron borer on textile machinery. Patience dies in Oldham in 1912; she is buried in Leek cemetery with Vernon who died in Leek in 1922.

Mary Henrietta Gillett
1859-1944

Mary Henrietta was born in Derby, the daughter of Frances Calvert Gillett and his wife, Mary Susanna. She stitched panel 23 of the facsimile of the Bayeux Tapestry when she lived at Duffield in Derbyshire. Her father was a wealthy civil and mining engineer and as befitting their status the family lived at Duffield Bank House, where they employed several staff including a cook, kitchen maid, housemaid and a waitress. Duffield Bank House, just four and a half miles from Derby, was a beautiful residence on the banks of the River Derwent. In 1886 Mary Gillett was present at the inauguration of a Primrose League at Duffield. The same year saw the Duffield branch of the Girls Friendly Society hold their annual festival at Duffield Bank House where prizes were awarded for needlework.

Right
Duffield Bank House

Right
Richard Clay Gillett, Mary's brother

When he died in 1895 Frances Gillett was a very wealthy man leaving an estate worth £134,000. His wife paid for a stained glass window, designed by Charles Eamer Kempe, to be installed in St Alkmund's Church in Duffield as a memorial to her husband.

After her father died Mary lived with her mother in the family home, but after the death of her mother she moved to Yeovil where she lived alone employing a cook and a housemaid. Mary never married and died in Yeovil in 1944.

Mary Adeline Gwynne
1858-1933

Mary was born in Rotherham, the daughter of John and Marianne Jones, her father was a Welshman and a Wesleyan Minister. As a child Mary lived in Yorkshire, Cornwall, Lancashire, Staffordshire and Cheshire. She married Clement Thomas Gwynne, a Leek solicitor, in 1882 at Macclesfield. Clement Gwynne worked for Challinor and Shaw; he was a partner in the firm from 1903. Frederick D Wardle, Thomas and Elizabeth Wardle's son, had also worked as a solicitor at the firm and would have been a colleague of Clement Gwynne. In 1895 they are both listed in the salary ledger when Clement earned £275 per year and Frederick Wardle just £50. In 1891 Clement was chairman of the Extension Lectures Committee which were held in the Art Gallery at the Nicholson Institute and also a member of the Leek High School for Girls Council.

In 1884, Mary with her husband and baby son moved into the newly erected Westwood Villas on Westwood Road in Leek. An advertisement in the Leek Times describes the villas as "commanding romantic and extensive views, embracing Rudyard Vale and the Roches [sic]". Each house had a porch and entrance hall, two reception rooms, kitchen, scullery, bathroom and w.c. on the ground floor with six bedrooms, bathroom, w.c. and linen closet above. The houses had excellent cellars, well laid out gardens and carriageway drives planted with choice trees. Clearly the villas were desirable residences and well beyond the finances of most working class people in the town. The villas still stand in Westwood Road, the Gwynne's home is now known as 100, Westwood Road.

Mary and Clement had two daughters and two sons, their daughter, Nora died in Leek aged fifteen and their son, Herbert Llewellyn was killed in action on the Somme in 1916. Their daughter, Dora, worked for Challinor and Shaw as an accountant and died a spinster in Leek in 1996. Clement Wansborough Gwynne, their surviving son, had a distinguished career in the

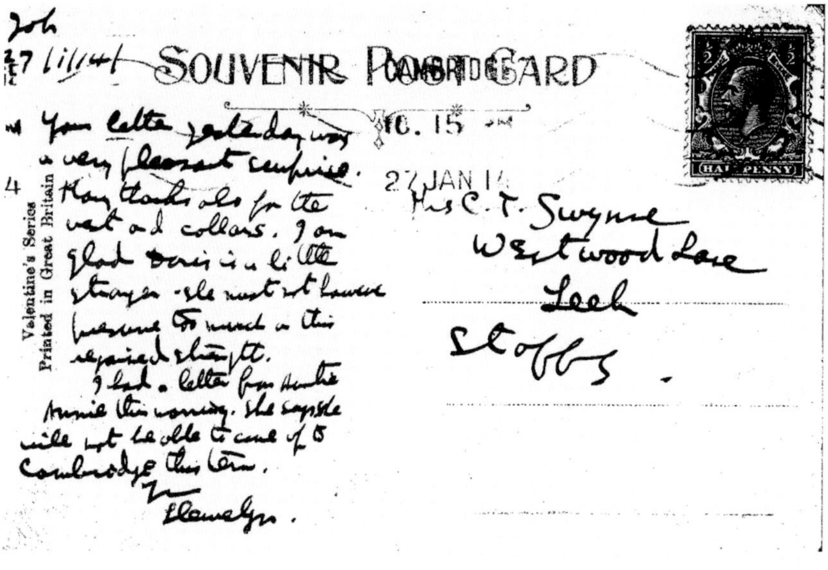
SOUVENIR POST CARD

Valentine's Series
Printed in Great Britain

CAMBRIDGE
10.15 AM
27 JAN 14

Your letter yesterday was a very pleasant surprise. Many thanks also for the vest and collars. I am glad Doris is a little stronger - she must not however presume too much on this regained strength.
I had a letter from Auntie Annie this morning. She says she will not be able to come up to Cambridge this term.
Llewelyn.

Mrs C. T. Gwynne
Westwood Lane
Leek
Staffs.

Right
Postcard sent from Mary Gwynne's son, who died in WW1

Right
Detail from cushion cover in 'Tile design' stitched by Mary Gwynne for her home

Right
Detail from a long border, possibly for a curtain, stitched by Mary Gwynne

Indian Civil Service. When he died, in 1929, his obituary in the local press commented on his magnificent career spent in the interests of the British Empire.

Not surprisingly the Gwynne's were Wesleyan Methodists and Mary's husband was a prominent figure in the Leek Wesleyan Methodist Circuit. In 1903 Clement lectured on 'Self Education' at a meeting of the Leek Wesley Guild in West Street School. They were both staunch Liberals, Clement had been both secretary and registration agent for the Leek Division Liberal Association and Mary had served as the secretary of the Leek Women's Liberal Association.

As the wife of a respected solicitor Mary accompanied her husband to public functions. The Gwynnes are pictured in the grounds of the Leek Cottage Hospital, in 1898, with other prominent townsfolk including Thomas Wardle. In 1920, Mary Gwynne attended Leek Girls High School's annual speech day and distribution of prizes at the Town Hall. She moved a vote of thanks to the presenter of the prizes. Mary Gwynne's stitched panel 24 of the facsimile of the Bayeux tapestry, when she was a member of Leek Embroidery Society, and also embroidered domestic pieces for her home throughout her life.

Elizabeth Haynes
1828 – 1916

Elizabeth was the daughter of Henry Haynes and his wife Hannah, nee Getliffe. Elizabeth lived with her parents at 10 Union Street in Leek and continued to live in this house after both her parents had died. In 1881, three years after the death of her father, Elizabeth is still in Union Street and is living on income derived from property. Although Henry Haynes was a retired builder, he had also worked as a joiner and had employed nine men. Many Leek builders owned the houses which they had built and derived an income from renting them so Elizabeth most probably inherited property from her father enabling her to live on the rental income. She moved from Union Street to a town house in Queen Street where she was a boarder. Then in her 70s she lived on her own in one of the Carr Almshouses in Fountain Street and finally as a boarder again in Spring Gardens. Elizabeth was the only member of her family to remain in Leek as several of her siblings died young and three of her brothers left Leek to begin a new life in Australia. Elizabeth Haynes stitched panel 15 of the facsimile.

Right
The Carr almshouses in Fountain Street

Beatrice Lavington
1868-1892

Beatrice Lavington lived in Leek for just a few years but while in the town she stitched panel 21 of the facsimile of the Bayeux Tapestry. She was born in Lambeth in 1868, the daughter of George and Frances Lavington. Beatrice's father was a stockbroker who had died in 1878. Shortly after his death his widow moved to Hugo Street in Leek with her son Walter and daughter Beatrice. Walter had secured a position as the manager of a silk mill in the town. The silk mill was most probably that of Alsop, Downes & Spilsbury in New Street as Walter Lavington's uncle was Benjamin Spilsbury, a partner in the Leek mill. Alsop, Downes and Spilsbury operated a silk mill in Huggin Lane in London as well as the mill in Leek. They manufactured sewing silks, braids and trimmings. Beatrice married Francis William Way, a woollen merchant, in Leek in 1887 and moved to Streatham with him. They had a daughter, Sylvia, born there in 1889. Sadly, Beatrice died in Streatham aged just 24 in 1892.

Anne Mills Lowe
1832 -1892

Anne Lowe was the daughter of George Nall, a printer, bookseller and stationer who operated in Leek, initially from Sheepmarket and then from Stanley Street. The property, where Anne spent most of her childhood and all of her married life, is now 'Den Engel' a Belgian bar. George Nall was well regarded in Leek and was the first churchwarden of St Luke's Church; he also planted the lime trees around the church. His daughter, Elizabeth, was the first person to be married in this new church in 1848. During the wardenship of George Nall the East window was put in and as some stained glass was left over it was presented to him by the makers. George inserted this glass in a fanlight over the Nall's front door in Stanley Street where it can still be seen.
Anne Nall married William Lowe, a wine merchant, in 1867 and together they operated the business from her former home at 11-13, Stanley Street. Anne embroidered panel 16 of the Bayeux Tapestry while living in Stanley Street.

Above
Anne Mills Lowe's name stitched on to panel 16 of the facsimile of the Bayeux Tapestry

Right
Anne Mills Lowe

Above
Den Engel, a Belgian bar, operates from the premises which was once the home and wine merchant's shop of the Lowe family

Right
Stained glass with the initials of George Nall, Den Engel's

William Lowe, Anne's husband, used Anne's inheritances from her father and her brother to finance his business dealings which was a source of considerable annoyance to Anne as he always overstretched himself and was often in financial difficulties. At one time, in addition to his wine merchant business, William Lowe had the Cattle Market Inn at the bottom of Fountain Street, the Nag's Head in Mill Street and the Black's Head at the bottom of the Market Place. Anne often writes in her diary of her dismay concerning her husband's debts and mentions his creditors, which included Thomson's, the brewery, and an old family servant who had lent her husband money.

In 1882 bankruptcy proceedings were initiated against him when he was both a wine merchant of Stanley Street and innkeeper of the King William IV in Church Street. Anne did not like her husband keeping public houses in addition to his wine merchant business as she felt that many people were "against those who sell intoxicating liquor". This may be why Anne and her daughters often attended temperance meetings in the town!

In 1889, William Lowe had been asked to put an advertisement in St Luke's Parish Magazine which had appeared on the front page. The Lowe family was surprised and hurt to be informed that there had been many objections to it and that Enoch Hill, the printer, dare not put it in again. Anne and her daughters felt snubbed and insulted.

Anne Lowe's diary reveals her strong religious beliefs; she regularly attended church services and was involved with many church social activities. She taught Sunday school at All Saints and supported church activities at St Luke's and St Edward's.

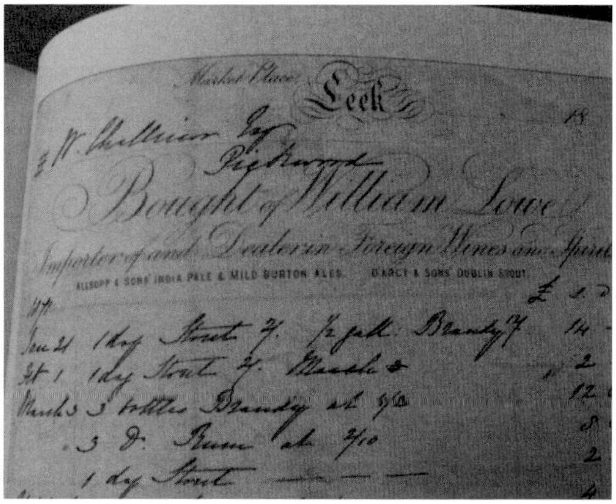

Market Place, Leek

Bought of William Lowe

Importer of and Dealer in Foreign Wines and Spirits

ALLSOPP & SONS' INDIA PALE & MILD BURTON ALES. D'ARCY & SONS' DUBLIN STOUT.

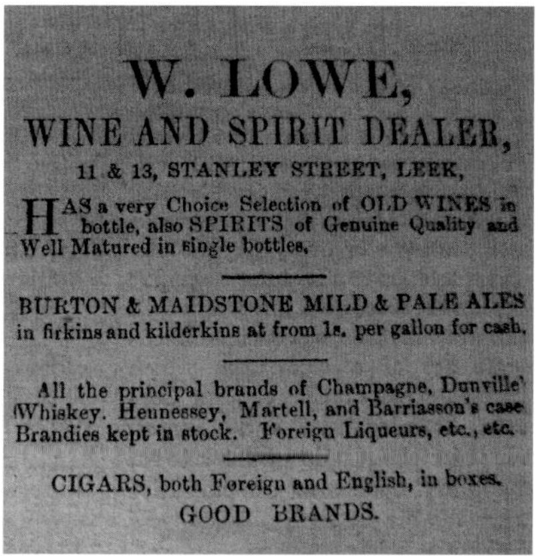

W. LOWE,

WINE AND SPIRIT DEALER,

11 & 13, STANLEY STREET, LEEK,

HAS a very Choice Selection of OLD WINES in bottle, also SPIRITS of Genuine Quality and Well Matured in single bottles.

BURTON & MAIDSTONE MILD & PALE ALES in firkins and kilderkins at from 1s. per gallon for cash.

All the principal brands of Champagne, Dunville' Whiskey. Hennessey, Martell, and Barriasson's case Brandies kept in stock. Foreign Liqueurs, etc., etc.

CIGARS, both Foreign and English, in boxes. GOOD BRANDS.

Above, left
Trade bill for William Lowe (Ann's husband) itemising wine and spirits purchased by William Challinor from Pickwood Hall

Above, right
William Lowe advert

Right
William Lowe's premises in Stanley Street

Right
Anne Lowe's brooch which she had made from the money she received when the facsimile of the Bayeux Tapestry was sold to Reading

Anne Lowe was extremely sensitive about her social standing in Leek, her diary records her dismay when she felt she had been snubbed at a tea party by Mrs George Wardle (the wife of Thomas Wardle's brother). She felt that she had been reminded of her presumption and bitterly reflects on past intimacies with the Wardle families of both Leek and Leekbrook. She records in her diary that since she was a young woman "the George Wardle's have gone up and I have gone down". As George Wardle was an executor of her father's will it would appear to confirm the former close relationship between the families. Indeed Anne's diary records that Martha Phoebe Wardle, George Wardle's daughter, had been her friend before her marriage but had dropped her after she married William Lowe. Anne Lowe refers in her diary to Mary E Wardle another "dear friend" who had died in 1860. This was Mary Eliza Wardle who was Elizabeth Wardle's younger sister.

Obviously Anne Lowe had a strong connection to the Wardle family before her marriage and although she believed that she had been cut off by them when she married William Lowe it is difficult to confirm this as Ann herself was a needlewoman who stitched for the Leek Embroidery Society, her daughter Beatrice Ellen (Nellie) was the secretary of the Society and her daughter Sarah Katherine (Katy) was Thomas Wardle's secretary.

Right
Back of the brooch

Anne and William Lowe had five daughters and a son; all the children were sent away to school at various establishments. Her daughters, Nellie and Katy, who both became secretaries, attended a college at Westbury on Trym near Clifton and her daughter Alice was a graduate of Newnham College, Cambridge before working as a teacher. Only Alice married, the other girls remained spinsters and after the death of their father became wine merchants at the shop in Stanley Street; they also kept The King William IV in Church Street. Anne's only son went to Canada where he died in 1921.
Anne Lowe died in Leek in 1897.

Elizabeth Valentine Lunn (nee Littlewood)
1847- 1933

Elizabeth Valentine Littlewood spent her early years in Armthorpe in Yorkshire where her father, John, farmed 850 acres. John was an affluent farmer who employed ten labourers and several indoor servants. John Littlewood must have been a prosperous man as he was able to retire from farming before his fiftieth birthday and move with his family to Hull. Elizabeth married Richard Lunn in Howden in 1876; he came from Bromley in Kent and had been working as a silver engraver in Chelsea. After they married Richard and Elizabeth lived in Nether Hallam in Sheffield where Richard worked as an artist in oil and water colour. Presumably Elizabeth was kept busy caring for their two small children as she has no occupation listed on the 1881 census return but ten years later, when the family have moved to Litchurch in Derby, she is working as a teacher of art embroidery. While she was living in Derby she is reputed to have taught at the Leek School of Embroidery. Several women from Derby helped to stitch the facsimile of the Bayeux Tapestry as did Elizabth Lunn, perhaps she was the link between Derby and the Leek Embroidery Society. When the Lunns lived in Derby Richard was the art director at the Royal Crown Derby Porcelain Company. He was well known for designing 'The Gladstone Service' which was presented to William Gladstone in 1883 by the Liberal Working Men of Derby. By the turn of the century the Lunns had moved to Chiswick as Richard had secured a position as a pottery and ceramics instructor at the Royal College of Art in London, a position he held until at least 1911. He also taught evening classes in pottery at Camberwell School of Art from 1908 until his death in 1915. When Elizabeth Lunn moved to London with her husband and two daughters they lived in a large house in Woodstock Road, after the death of her husband Elizabeth lived at this house until she died in 1933. There is no evidence to prove that Elizabeth worked as an embroidery teacher in London but she may well have done so. She would have certainly lived an interesting life accompanying her husband to exhibitions, meetings and other events and was most probably in the audience when her husband addressed the Art Workers Guild in 1912.

Dora, the Lunn's youngest daughter inherited her parents artistic talents, she studied ceramics at Camberwell School of Art and set up the Ravenscourt Pottery at Hammersmith in 1916.

Emily Parker (later Campion)
1851-1939

Emily, the daughter of Frederick and Ann Parker, was born in Derby. Her father, who was born in London, was a chemist and druggist whose business premises were in the Corn Market in Derby where he employed two apprentices. Tragically, Emily's mother had died when Emily was only eight years old leaving her husband with six children. Frederick and his children moved to 11 North Parade in Derby where Frederick died in 1863 when Emily was thirteen. Her eldest sister, Sarah, who was then twenty years of age, became the head of the family. The Parker family was not poor as the orphaned children lived on income derived from the interest on dividends. Sarah Parker, Emily's sister, came to Leek after she married William Berresford who was the vicar of St Luke's parish church. Emily was staying with them in the vicarage in 1881 where she came into contact with a new young curate named Alfred Campion. Both Emily and Alfred were involved with young people in the church guilds. In early 1887 the Parish Magazine records that the young men in the guild were making great efforts to complete 'the furniture for the holy table' while the maidens, through the efforts of Emily Parker, had contributed ten shillings in six

Right
St Luke's Vicarage

Above
St Luke's Church in the snow

months towards a supply of fresh flowers. While she lived in Leek with her sister and brother-in-law Emily stitched panel 11 of the facsimile of the Bayeux Tapestry.

Alfred Campion had left Leek in 1887 when he was ordained as the vicar of Sneyd in Burslem but he returned to Leek in 1893 to marry Emily at St Luke's Church. The newly married couple, who were both in their forties, lived in Burslem before moving to Kirton in Nottinghamshire where they lived in the rectory. Emily's husband became the rural dean of the parish of Tuxford in 1917. The Campion's spent their final years in West Avenue in Derby.

Eliza McKenzie (Lizzie)
1860- 1911

Eliza, who was always known as Lizzie, was one of ten children born to John William Harris McKenzie and his wife Marianne. Her father was a physician and surgeon who initially practiced in Penkridge and her grandfather had been a leading planter in Jamaica.

Eliza and her elder siblings were all born in Penkridge before the family moved to Cheadle in Staffordshire in 1862. The McKenzie family moved into Daisy Bank House in Cheadle, a spacious property now a nursing home, which had previously been the home of John Colclough Bourne. John Bourne, who was John Mckenzie's uncle, had been a physician and surgeon in Cheadle until his death in 1861.

John W H McKenzie, Lizzie's father, had held the offices of Medical Officer and Public Vaccinator for Cheadle for over twenty-five years. At Daisy Bank he employed domestic servants including a governess and a nurse to look after the younger children. Lizzie and her sisters never had to work for a living but her brothers all had professional occupations. Ernest McKenzie, Lizzie's younger brother, took over from their father and was a respected Cheadle physician and surgeon who gave a lifetime's service to the area. He served on the Parish Council and was a governor of local schools; the McKenzie Secondary School in Cheadle was named after him in recognition of all his work. When he died, in 1939, Ernest McKenzie left a trust fund in his will to assist the pupils of Cheadle Schools into further education.

Eliza, as the daughter and sister of men who played prominent roles in the activities of Cheadle, would have supported them by attending functions in the community. After the death of their father, in 1899, Eliza and her elder sister, Ada Mary, moved to Hampshire where they lived together firstly in Eversley and later in 'The Firs" a spacious cottage in Hook. The two spinster sisters had private means.

The Pattinson Sisters

Alice Pattinson
1864 – 1936

Florence Pattinson
1866 – 1940

Alice Mary and Florence Pattinson were the daughters of Thomas Pattinson and his wife Margaret nee Smith. Their father was a prosperous silk mercer and draper whose business premises were in Mill Street in Macclesfield where he employed twenty six labourers [sic]. By 1871 the Pattinson family had moved to Walker Street in Macclesfield where Thomas employed seven assistants, five apprentices, six work girls and a porter. When Thomas retired the family moved to the Lake House on Old Leek Road in Sutton. Alice Pattinson never married, she lived with her father in the Lake House until he died moving some time later to Alton where she lived and died at Dimblecroft.

Right
Lake House

Alice was the only Pattinson sibling to stay with her parents, her sisters Helena and Florence left Macclesfield to study at Newnham College. They both converted to Roman Catholicism much to their father's disapproval. It is known that he sent Florence to Dr Stubbs, the Bishop of Oxford, in the hope that he would deter her. However, the independently minded Pattinson sisters were not swayed from their convictions. Helena was received into the Roman Catholic Church at the Assumption Convent in Kensington in 1887 and she entered Stanbrook Abbey in Worcestershire where she was given the name Sister Barbara. According to Robert Ferguson in his book *The Short Sharp Life of T.E.Hulme*, she was a gifted icon painter and a translator of catholic texts. In the 1891 and 1901 census returns she is listed as the English mistress at Stanbrook Abbey. Alice Pattinson's younger sister, Florence, also became a nun at Stanbrook where she was known as Dame Ursula; she was the drawing mistress there. At Stanbrooke Ursula (Florence), according to Robert Ferguson, was known for her beautiful mezzo-soprano voice. As well as teaching drawing she was a designer and embroiderer of vestments, a tapestry weaver and a designer of furniture for the abbey. Florence Pattinson stitched a panel of the facsimile of the Bayeux Tapestry as did her sister Alice, her sister-in-law Jennie Smith and her aunt Ann Smith.

The Pearson Sisters

Margaret Maude Pearson (later Worthington)
1859 – 1927

Florence May Pearson
born 1864

Margaret and Florence Pearson, who both worked on the facsimile of the Bayeux Tapestry, were born at Gatcombe House in Littlehempston, near Totnes. Their father, Thomas Pearson, described himself as a 'gentleman with funded property'. The family lived a life of luxury supported by numerous servants although the sisters would probably not remember this impressive house as Thomas Pearson took his family to Birkenhead when the girls were very young. This move was the result of a bad investment which brought him close to ruin but Thomas was not defeated and began an insurance business in Birkenhead which proved so successful that the family was able to move to London in 1879. Indeed Thomas Pearson's business prospered to the extent that when he died in 1902 he left an estate in excess of £105,000.

Right
Haregate Hall, Leek

Below, right
Ernest Andrew Worthington

Below, left
Margaret Pearson

Margaret Pearson married Ernest Andrew Worthington, a Leek silk manufacturer, at Barnes in 1880 and lived with him at Ball Haye Hall for a short time before moving to Haregate Hall. As the wife of a wealthy silk manufacturer she would have been invited to many social activities in the town attending garden parties, balls, plays and supporting charity events with other ladies within her social circle. Ernest Worthington died in 1896 leaving Margaret with six children including a baby son. Margaret married again two years later to John Wilson, a retired linen merchant, and lived with him at Hillesdon on Mount Road in Leek, then a newly built house and now a rest home.
Margaret stitched part of panel 11 of the facsimile of the Bayeux Tapestry when she was married to Ernest Worthington and living at Haregate Hall. Some years earlier her husband's sisters, Rose and Alice Worthington, had stitched part of the Pelican altar frontal for St Luke's Church. A link was forged with the Wardle family when Thomas and Elizabeth's daughter, Margaret, married Philip Worthington, Ernest's younger brother.

Florence Pearson lived in Putney when she helped to stitched panel 9 of the facsimile of the Bayeux Tapestry. No doubt she visited her sister at Haregate Hall on many occasions and would have been aware of the work of the Leek Embroidery Society. She would have had to liaise with Ann Smith from Endon, a village a few miles from Leek, who also stitched part of panel 9 so she may have stitched while in Leek. The Pearson girls were also connected to Leek through their mother, Lucy Ann Clover, who was the niece of Frances Ann Clover who had married Anthony Ward yet another Leek silk manufacturer. The Clover family were very wealthy ship builders in Birkenhead.

Margaret Ritchie
1827 – 1910

Margaret Ritchie, the daughter of John and Mary Ann Ritchie, was born at Upper Tean where her father was a general practitioner and surgeon. She lived with her parents in Upper Tean until her father died when she and her mother moved into Leek where her brother, John James Ritchie, was working as Leek's medical officer. He lived at 31 Ball Haye Street an imposing Georgian property which stood in its own grounds and is now divided into apartments known as Stockwell Mews. Margaret and her mother lived just a short distance away in a town house at the bottom of Queen Street. John James Ritchie and Richard Turnock were both trustees of the Leek and Moorlands Temperance Society who had purchased the Meeting House and land in Union Street in 1864, which afterwards became the Temperance Hall. The Ritchie's worshipped at the Congregational Church and were strong supporters of the Temperance Movement.

After her brother's wife had died Margaret Ritchie moved into his home at 31 Ball Haye Street to run his household with the help of a cook and a housemaid. In 1901, John James Ritchie married Mary Ann Sugden, the daughter of William Sugden, whose distinctive architecture dominates Leek.

Margaret attended drawing and painting classes at the Mechanics Institute in Russell Street in the 1870s and was connected with the Leek Embroidery Society from its early years. She was one of the women who worked Tussur silk in Indian designs displayed at an exhibition in the Temperance Hall in 1881. Both Margaret Ritchie and Elizabeth Wardle allowed their names to be used as references for a proposed Art Emporium in Leek which was advertised in the *Leek Times* in 1884; a proposal which unfortunately never came to fruition. Miss Ritchie was an honorary member of Leek's Amateur Musical Society where her brother was also a vocal member and a former president. She died in Hayling Island in 1910 leaving her estate to a nephew.

Margaret stitched panel 6 of the facsimile of the Bayeux Tapestry.

Above
31 Ball Haye Street

Smith Family

Ann Smith
1822-1901

Jane Smith (Jennie)
1851 - 1924

Many of the Leek needlewomen were related and Ann Smith was the aunt of Charles Philip Smith whose wife, Jennie, also helped to stitch the Facsimile of the Bayeux Tapestry. Interestingly Ann was also the aunt of sisters Alice and Florence Pattinson (see pages 67-68) as Ann's sister Margaret had married Thomas Pattinson. Confusingly, Ann Smith's elder sister, Catherine, had married Samuel Young, who was Elizabeth Wardle's uncle. These close relationships are not unexpected in a small market town.
Ann Smith was the daughter of Thomas and Catherine Smith, her father was a yeoman farmer in Endon. Ann, a spinster, lived with her younger brother, George, a solicitor, at Endon Bank after the death of her parents. Ann was a woman of independent means, a fund holder, who was able to use money left to her for her support. After her brother George died, glass by Morris & Co. was installed in the east window of St Luke's church at Endon in his memory. Ann's elder brother, Thomas, paid for the installation of a north aisle in the church in 1899 in memory of his wife. The Smiths of Endon were a wealthy family who supported their local church; when George Smith died he left a considerable estate. He gave £200 to the church, so that the interest could be distributed among the poor living within one mile of Endon village. Ann and her sister, Mary, stitched the purple altar frontal for St Luke's church at Endon and Ann stitched part of the facsimile of the Bayeux Tapestry.

Right
St Luke's Church, Endon

Above, left
Altar Frontal for St Luke's Church, Endon stitched by Ann Smith and her sister, Mary

Above, right
Detail from the Altar Frontal

Right
The White House,
Alton

Jennie, as she was usually known was the daughter of Charles Hancock who was a saddler and harness maker in the village of Yoxall. In 1879 she married Charles Philip Smith in London; he was Ann Smith's nephew. Charles Smith, born in Alton, was a surveyor and landowner. Charles and Jennie lived in London in the 1880s and Jennie has entered her address as London on the panel of the facsimile of the Bayeux Tapestry which she stitched. Charles and Jennie retired to Bournemouth but also lived at the White House in the village of Alton, not far from Leek. The White House had previously been the home of his father and was later the home of Barnet Young, Elizabeth Wardle's cousin.

Margaret Eliza Watson
1846 – 1926

Margaret Watson was the wife of William Saddington Watson, a silk manufacturer, whose mill still stands on the corner of Brook Street and London Street in Leek. William Watson was in partnership with his brother Charles and traded as Watson & Company, silk throwers and manufacturers. The brothers were also part of the Leek Spun Silk Manufacturing Company as was Thomas Wardle. Yet again the Leek Embroidery Society is shown to be a family affair; in this case Margaret's sister-in-law was also a member of the society.

Right
Margaret Watson
(nee Russell)

Margaret was the daughter of John and Christina Russell, her father was a silk manufacturer who employed 300 hands at his Britannia silk mill in Leek in 1861. The Russell family lived in a large house in Spout Street (now St Edward Street) in Leek which many years later became the home of Thomas and Elizabeth Wardle. Britannia Mill together with the machinery and the goodwill of the business was sold in 1870, after bankruptcy proceedings, and the Russell family moved to a terraced house in Ford Street. Not surprisingly Margaret and her younger sister, Mary, were then both working, Margaret as a teacher and Mary as a governess.

Right
The former Watson's mill in Brook Street

Right
Watson trade bill

Margaret married W. S. Watson at Endon in 1875 when she wore a grey silk dress and a light blue bonnet over which was thrown a white veil. Young ladies who were members of the bride's day school class strewed flowers down the aisle as the wedding party left the church. The report of Margaret's marriage in the *Leek Times* reflects on her amiable disposition and many virtues. Margaret had won the affection of the whole village of Endon where she assisted with decorations and musical entertainments. The marriage was celebrated at the Rudyard Hotel, near to Rudyard Lake, by the Watson employees, About 250 partook of the liberal refreshments, served on the green in front of the hotel, and afterwards rambled about the grounds by the lake while others took part in the dancing and sports which included sack races. The Watson brothers joined in the sporting contests while the new Mrs. Watson and her sister distributed the prizes.

When Margaret Watson died at Southfields, Leek, in her 81st year, her obituary referred to her large circle of friends. Several members of the Wardle family attended her funeral as did Mrs Warren who was a neighbour. Mrs Warren stitched the beautiful altar frontals for St Chad's Church at Longsdon.

Mary Edith Watson nee Challinor
1858-1898

Mary Watson was the daughter of William and Elizabeth Challinor and the sister-in-law of Margaret Eliza Watson. Both her father and grandfather were solicitors with lucrative practices in Leek. Mary spent her childhood at Pickwood Hall on the outskirts of town where she and her siblings enjoyed idyllic days. The Challinor family worshipped at St Luke's and Mary often took part in amateur concerts there.
She married Charles Watson at St Luke's Church in 1884. The Watson family also had a strong association with St Luke's as Charles Watson was the churchwarden there at the turn of the century.

Right
Mrs Charles Watson

Above
Watson and Challinor wedding, William Challinor can be seen seated to the left of the bride

Charles Watson was a wealthy silk manufacturer whose silk mill stood at the corner of Brook Street and London Street. When he died in 1923 he left £13,792, an indication of the wealth of a prosperous Leek silk manufacturer.

Before her marriage, Mary was educated in Leek, Brighton and London. She was a patron of both the Cruso Nursing Association and the Leek Charitable Organization Society. Mary Edith was one of the Embroidery Society women who came from privileged backgrounds, it is highly unlikely that she ever undertook paid commissions. Her only known work is that of panel 12 of the facsimile of the Bayeux tapestry.

Mary Edith Watson died aged forty at Woodview in Leek leaving two young sons. A wooden chancel screen was erected in St Luke's Church in her memory and that of her father. Her funeral service was held at St Luke's Church where two of the bearers were Thomas Wardle and his son Arthur. Mary Edith was spared the tragedy of the death of her eldest son Charles Challinor Watson who was killed in France in 1917.

The ‘Four Kings’ Altar Frontal

Background Image
Detail form the ‘Four Kings’ Altar Frontal

ETh ELBERT REX
FATHERS

Above
The 'Four Kings' Altar Frontal

Right
An extract from *Leek Parish Church Magazine* dated November 1895

On the Sunday after S. Edward's Day a most beautiful Dedication Altar Cloth was presented to our Church by Mrs. Wardle. As the Church is dedicated in the name of S. Edward four kings are represented on the frontal, viz: King Edward himself in the panel on the south side, and the first Christian Saxon King, Ethelberi, on the north side. The two centre panels are filled with figures of Kings David and Solomon. On the bottom of the frontal is the scroll "Kings shall be thy nursing fathers," and on the super frontal are the words "King of Kings and Lord of Lords." I believe the original conception of the King Frontal was due to the donor, who carried out the design in needlework with the help of the Leek Embroidery Society, after the design had been drawn by Mr. J. S. Rigby under the direction of his father-in-law, Mr. G. Young Wardle. The Frontal will probably be one of the chief monuments of the needlework of this century and that it should be presented to the Leek Parish Church is one more mark of the love of the donor for the Church which is to so many the Church of their fathers.

The Embroidery Society has done much good work, but it will not easily surpass the King Frontal. I am told that the figures are the first which have been worked in Leek, and that King Ethelbert and a portion of King Edward have been elaborated by the skilful fingers of Miss Charlotte Robinson.

Above
Back row left to right; Mary Ann Bishop, Beatrice Ellen Lowe (Nellie), Frances Christina Redfern (Cissie), Sarah Catherine Price (Kitty)
Middle row left to right; Mary Alice Garside (Molly), Ann Cartwright (Queenie), Ellen Vigrass (Nellie), Annie Rowley
Front Row left to right; Annie Redfern, Nellie McDonough, Annie Brunt

Several of the girls pictured with Elizabeth Wardle on this photograph, dated 1888, reputedly worked on the 'Four Kings' green altar frontal which is permanently displayed in the parlour at St Edward's church in Leek. An entry in *Leek Parish Church Magazine* states that the frontal was presented to the church by Elizabeth Wardle in 1895. It was designed by J S Rigby directed by his father-in-law George Young Wardle. George Young Wardle was Elizabeth Wardle's brother who worked as William Morris' business manager. His daughter Mary, known as Kitten, had married John Scarratt Rigby in London in 1889.

Mary Ann Bishop
1866-1933

Above
Mary Ann Bishop

Mary Ann, the eldest daughter of Thomas and Emma Bishop, was born in Leekbrook. Thomas Bishop was Thomas Wardle's cousin as their mothers were the sisters Martha and Mary Darlington. Martha had married Alexander Bishop while Mary had married Joshua Wardle who was Thomas Wardle's father. Mary Ann was one of five girls born to Thomas and Emma Bishop; the three eldest girls were born at Leekbrook where their father worked for Joshua Wardle & Co. as a silk warehouseman. In the early 1870s the Bishop family moved to Leek where the two youngest girls were born. Mary Ann's uncle, James Bishop, worked for the Wardle's as a cashier at the Leekbrook dye-works. Alexander Bishop, Mary Ann's grandfather was also an employee at Joshua Wardle & Co.

When Thomas Bishop died, in 1879, at the age of forty, his wife was left with five girls to support. Mary Ann was then thirteen years old and her youngest sister only four. After her father died, Mary and her mother worked in a silk mill as pattern card makers. This involved making cards displaying samples of ribbons, silks, braids etc. for travellers to take out to prospective purchasers. Mary Ann's sister, Sarah, aged 12, worked as a half time silk winder, spending half a day at school and half a day working in the mill. It would seem that Thomas Wardle was not giving any financial help to his cousin's widow and children at this time but in 1888 Mary Ann is pictured with Elizabeth Wardle, presumably at the School of Embroidery, where she was taught to stitch and was able to earn her living as an embroiderer.

The Bishop family lived in Rosebank Street when they first moved to Leek and later moved to Grosvenor Street. Both these streets were part of the parish of St Luke which is why this church has several examples of Mary Ann's embroidery. She stitched the Agnus Dei frontal with matching pulpit and lectern falls, bookmarkers and alms bags for the church and is believed to have stitched super frontals for St Anne's church in Millersdale.

Right
The Agnus Dei frontal for St Luke's church stitched by Mary Ann

Right
Details from the Agnus Dei frontal

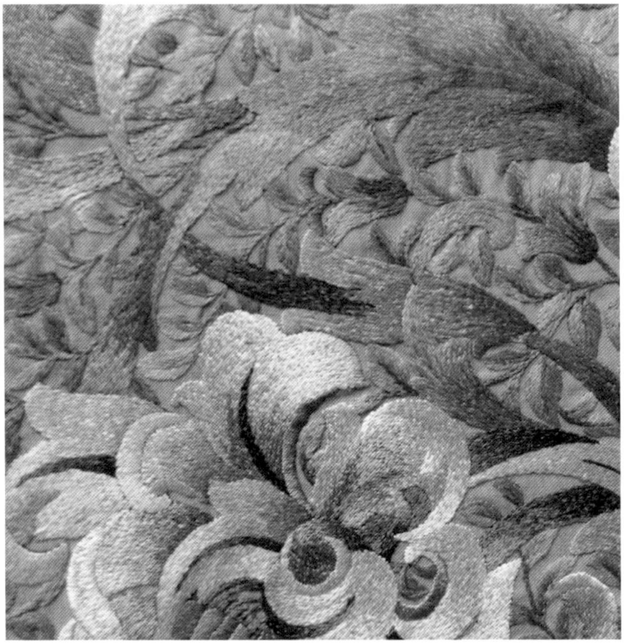

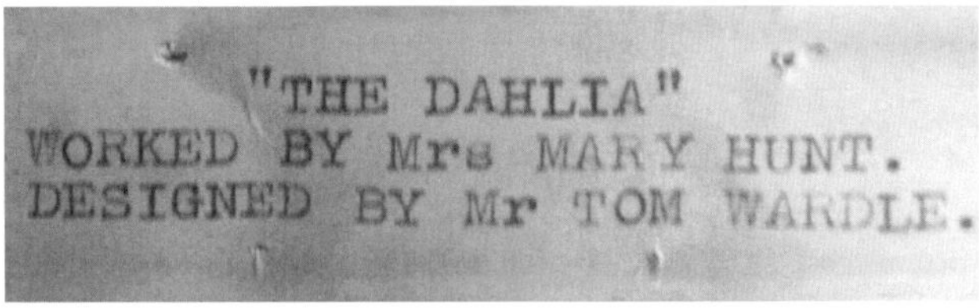

Above
Detail from the Dahlia fire screen stitched by Mary Ann Hunt (nee Bishop)

Above, right
The Dahlia fire screen designed by Tom Wardle, son of Thomas and Elizabeth. For many years this fire screen stood in the offices at the Leekbrook dye-works

Above
Details from the fire Screen

Above, right
Mary Ann stitched this fire screen for her home

Mary Ann married Edward Hunt in 1894 at St Luke's church and spent the rest of her life in Leek. She continued to embroider throughout her life; her descendants have several examples of her exquisite embroidery. Mary Ann died in Shirburn Road in 1933.

The Brunt Sisters

Annie Louise Brunt
1873 - 1957

Elizabeth Jane Brunt
1883-1966

Above
Annie Brunt as an embroidery pupil

Annie Brunt was born in Bolton in Lancashire where her father, Joseph, was working as a blacksmith. Joseph, however, came from the Staffordshire Moorlands and grew up at the Royal Cottage, a remote property on the Leek to Buxton Road, where his father worked as a farmer and publican. Annie's mother was a Lancashire lass who married Joseph Brunt in Blackburn in 1871. Joseph Brunt had connections with Lancashire as he had been a sergeant farrier in the Duke of Lancaster's Yeomanry later occupying a similar position in the Staffordshire Yeomanry. By 1881 Joseph had returned to his roots and Annie lived with her parents and siblings in Heathylee, a rural district of Leek Parish. Annie was one of Elizabeth Wardle's embroidery girls. She is identified as an art embroidery worker (trim) on the census return of 1891 indicating that Annie was working as a paid embroiderer at that time. The Brunt family became established at 7-9 St Edward Street in Leek where Joseph Brunt worked as a blacksmith for many years. The blacksmith's shop occupied one of the former stables of the George Hotel which stood on the corner of St Edward Street and Church Street. Interestingly this property was very near to Elizabeth Wardle's home so perhaps this could account for Annie Brunt being taken on as an embroidery pupil as her father may have looked after Thomas Wardle's horses.
Although Annie helped to stitch the 'Four Kings' frontal for St Edward's Church no records survive of other contributions that Annie may have made to the work of the Leek Embroidery Society, but in common with other needlewomen she most probably continued to embroider items for her home and family. In 1901 Annie married Harry Dishley who was a commercial

Below
The Blacksmith's shop at the top of St Edward Street where Joseph Brunt once plied his trade

traveller for a silk mill. Harry and Annie lived at 44 Westwood Terrace but later moved to Ivy Lea in Hartington Street. This house was described by a local estate agent as a "spacious and versatile four bedroomed late Victorian town house, a most attractive and sizeable property in a quiet, popular location". It would have been a very desirable residence and the Dishley family must have been financially secure to have been able to move there. Harry Dishley was a respected businessman having worked as a commercial traveller for William Milner & Sons for over forty years. His obituary, in 1938, reflects on his lifelong association with the Congregational Chapel in Derby Street and his membership of the Central Liberal Club and of Leek Golf Club. Annie Dishley (nee Brunt) died at The Cottage in Birchall Lane in Leek in 1957.

One of Annie Brunt's sisters was Elizabeth Jane Brunt who worked as a secretary in 1911. Evidence suggests that she is the Miss B Prunt who is recorded in *Kelly's Directory* in 1908 as the secretary of the Leek Embroidery Society and the School of Embroidery at 56 St Edward Street. The surname 'Prunt' is not known in Leek and is most likely a misprint. Elizabeth had been a schoolmistress before she became a secretary, the *Leek Annual* of 1898 records her as Bessie Brunt a pupil teacher at Leek Parish Church School.
Elizabeth (Bessie) Brunt was a spinster in 1911; but in 1916 she married Arthur Roberts, a raw silk salesman, at St Edward's church. During her life she had a long association with St Edward's church and was also an active member of the Girls Friendly Society helping to stitch the sanctuary carpet for the church in 1907. She was active in the Girl Guides Movement and had helped to train Guiders. She had been a member of Westwood Golf Club and later a member and captain at Leek Golf Club. She died at Shirburn House which still stands on the corner of Shirburn Road and Ashbourne Road. This substantial house, now divided into flats, was once

Right
Shirburn House

the home of Falkner Nicholson, from the wealthy Nicholson silk family. The Robert's family must have been relatively well off to have lived in this property.

The Brunt family continued as farriers and blacksmiths in St Edward Street until at least 1949.

Ann Cartwright
born 1869

Above
Ann (Queenie) Cartwright

Ann Cartwright, nicknamed Queenie, was born in Leek in 1869. Her father, Daniel Cartwright, was an ironmonger whose shop was located at 3 Sheep Market. Leek residents will remember these premises as Blakemore and Chell who were ironmongers there until 2005. Ann's mother was a member of the Whittles family who had a grocers shop nearby. Her uncle, Thomas Whittles, had a silk dyeing business at Wellington Mill in Strangman Street in Leek. He had been in partnership with Joseph Bentley whose daughter, Emma Jane, was also a member of the Leek Embroidery Society.

Daniel Cartwright was a quiet and unostentatious man his only public office being that of returning officer. Like Thomas Wardle he was a staunch conservative and a regular member of the congregation at St Edward's church.

Ann was an employee of the Leek Embroidery Society and a pupil at the Leek School of Embroidery. She describes her occupation as silk embroideress [sic] on the 1891 census return, when she was still living with her parents in Sheep Market.

In addition to her work on the 'Four Kings' altar frontal for St Edward's church, Ann embroidered panel 5 of the facsimile of the Bayeux Tapestry with Mary Ann Bishop, Mary Alice Garside and Patience Gater. In 1895, Ann married Evan Humphries before moving to live with him in Worcester where Evan worked as a printer, bookbinder, bookseller and general stationer.

Ann remained in Worcester and remarried there in 1924 to James Woodhead after her first husband had died. Her mother and two of her sisters moved to Rochdale and went into business as confectioners. Her eldest brother Sampson took over her father's ironmongery business in Leek and her brother, John, became a bank accountant in town.

Right
Cartwright's shop in
Sheep Market

Above
The entrance to
Cartwright's house
in Dog Lane

Right
Daniel Cartwright
seated on the left

Mary Alice (Molly) Garside
1869 – 1920

Above
Mary Alice (Molly) Garside

Molly was born in Warslow, a village in the Staffordshire Moorlands, she was the daughter of Adam and Harriet Garside. Her father came from Yorkshire but her mother Harriet Green, was a native of Warslow. Harriet married Adam Garside in Leek in 1865 and they had three children. As a young child Molly lived with her mother and her maternal grandparents at Top o' the Town in Warslow. Later Harriet and her children moved into Leek to live with her husband's parents at 2 Ford Street where her father-in-law, John Garside, had a woollen draper's shop. Molly's father, Adam Garside, led a somewhat itinerant lifestyle and is conspicuously absent from most census returns and is never recorded with the family. Glimpses of his life can be found in local court records which reveal that he was a joiner by trade. In 1880, Adam is in Bristol where he again appears in court records. Harriet Garside, Molly's mother worked as a dressmaker, as did Molly's elder sister, but Molly became one of Elizabeth Wardle's needlewomen and a paid employee of the society. Her descendants are aware of her connection with the Embroidery Society and have examples of her work. Molly helped to stitch the 'Four Kings' altar frontal which can be seen in St Edward's Church in Leek and she is recorded as an embroiderer on the 1891 census returns.

In 1894 she married Francis Billing in Leek when Francis was working as a solicitor's clerk. By 1901 Francis Billing had become the secretary to the Leek and Moorlands Building Society whose offices were located at 15 Stockwell Street. This was an advantageous position for a young family man and one that would have been financially rewarding. The Billing family prospered and moved to Abbotsfield, a large house in Buxton Road in Leek which was built for them. Francis and Molly had five children, tragically one of her sons died aged twelve and Molly was devastated when her eldest son Harold was killed in action on the Somme, a blow from which she never fully recovered.

Above, top left
The Billing family on the lawn at Abbotsfield

Above, bottom left
Molly in the countryside, right hand side of picture

Above, right
Molly with her family

Above
Detail of letter rack stitched by Molly Garside

Above, right
Needle case stitched by Molly Garside (this is not Leek Embroidery)

Right
The house and shop on the corner of Market Street. Once the home of the Garside family

Right
Brunswick Chapel in Market Street where Molly worshipped. A car park now stands on the site where the chapel stood

Molly Billing died, following an operation, in 1920. Her funeral service was held at Brunswick Chapel in Market Street where she had worshipped for most of her life and where she was a member of the sewing circle. Clara Bill sent a floral wreath on behalf of the Leek Embroidery Society and the mourners included Mrs Dishley, Roberts and Grace who all were connected with the Society.

Beatrice Helen Lowe
1868-1921

Above
Nellie Lowe

Nellie Lowe, as she was always known, was one of the daughters of William and Anne Lowe. She was educated privately finally leaving Clifton Ladies College in 1882. She and her sisters attended tea parties, temperance meetings, fund raisers and amateur theatrical entertainments with their mother. She was a member of the Old Church (St Edward's) working party and from 1895 until her death worked diligently for the Leek branch of the Soldiers and Sailors Families Association. This branch had been founded by Elizabeth Wardle who had worked for it throughout the Boer War. Nellie is pictured with Elizabeth Wardle's embroidery girls in 1888 and later helped to stitch the 'Four Kings' altar frontal.

There is no evidence to suggest that Nellie stitched any other embroideries and her main role was as the secretary of the Leek Embroidery Society and the Leek School of Embroidery. She held both these positions until at least 1901. After her father died, in 1903, she and her sisters continued to operate the family wine merchants business from the premises in Stanley Street where they also resided. They employed a manager at the King William IV public house in Church Street where they were still licensees in 1908. In common with other Embroidery Society members, Nellie and her sisters were members of the Leek branch of the Primrose League. This was an organization which supported Conservative candidates and as their father, William Lowe, had been a staunch conservative it is hardly surprising that his daughters were involved in the Leek branch named 'The Cruso Habitation'. Nellie did not marry and died in the Cottage Hospital in Leek after a severe operation. Her obituary in a local newspaper reports that although the operation had been successful it had left her "weak and unable to rally" resulting in her death from heart failure. Several members of the Wardle family from both Leek and Leekbrook attended her funeral at All Saints Church, as did several women who had been members of the Leek Embroidery Society. A floral tribute

Above
The Lowe Sisters, Nellie is bottom left and her sister Katherine (who was Thomas Wardle's secretary) is next to her (bottom centre)

Right
Nellie Lowe

was sent by Clara Bill representing Leek Embroidery Society and a cross was received conveying deepest regret from the family of the late Lady Wardle.

Nellie's mother, Anne Lowe, stitched a panel of the facsimile of the Bayeux Tapestry and her sister, Katherine, was Thomas Wardle's secretary.

The Meerbrook Nicholsons

Rose Nicholson
1839 – 1905

Rose was the wife of William Nicholson who was the vicar at St Matthew's church in Meerbrook for 28 years. Meerbrook is a rural village not far from Leek. The Nicholsons were living at the vicarage there when Richard Norman Shaw rebuilt the church, in 1873, and also designed an altar frontal for it. This frontal and others were stitched by Elizabeth Wardle and other local needlewomen.

The Nicholsons had spent the early years of their marriage at Horncastle in Lincolnshire, where William was the curate at St Mary's Church. Their eldest daughters, Jessie and Edith Maud, were born there. By 1867 William and family had moved to Onecote, near Leek .and in 1870 William became the vicar at Meerbrook. Dora, their youngest daughter was born in Meerbrook in 1871. When William Nicholson retired from the church he moved to Heathwood in London Road, Buxton with his wife and his spinster daughters. Rose Nicholson's only son, Wilfred, born when the family were at Onecote, followed his father's calling, becoming the curate at St Michael and All Angels church in Portsmouth, before undertaking a life at sea as a naval chaplain.

Rose Nicholson was a widow when she died in Swanage in 1905.

Edith Maud Nicholson
1864-1944

Edith Maud was living in the vicarage at Meerbrook when she and her mother helped to stitch the Four Kings frontal. She was a talented young woman who, apart from her needlework skills, wrote novels. In 1892 her novel was advertised in the Daily News, the Morning Post and the London Standard. Entitled *'Bent on Conquest'* the novel, published by Hurst and Blackett, was in three volumes. The Daily Telegraph reported that this was a story in which sentimental readers would rejoice. In *'Bibliotheca Staffordiensis'* published in 1894, she is recorded as having been educated at a Ladies Seminary in Stockport and in Geneva. It would seem that this young lady may have been sent to a finishing school.
After her parents died Edith Maud lived at West Lodge in St Johns Road, Buxton with her two unmarried sisters. The 1911 census return records the three middle aged sisters as having private means. When Edith Maud died in 1944 she left over £8,000 to her younger sister, Dora. Edith Maud is typical of many of the women who stitched altar frontals for local churches as members of the Leek Embroidery Society. Many of them were women of independent means, who never married, and who lived long lives.

Sarah Catherine (Kitty) Price
1863-1900

Above
Kitty Price, one of Elizabeth Wardle's needlewomen

Sarah was one of Elizabeth Wardle's embroiderers. Kitty, as she was known to her friends and family, was the daughter of Thomas Price and his wife, Sarah. Thomas Price, a Welshman, was a clerk and bookkeeper at Challinor's solicitor's office in Derby Street. The Price family lived in court 10 off Ashbourne Road. Although Kitty was an embroidery pupil she worked as a milliner and not as an embroiderer. As one of Elizabeth Wardle's needlewomen she helped to stitch the 'Four Kings' altar frontal for St Edward's church.

When she was twenty nine she married William Goostrey, a retired paper manufacturer and a man of means. He had been connected to the paper mill at Cheddleton for over twenty years. William Goostrey was 75 years old at the time of his marriage to Kitty at St Luke's church in Leek. He had been living in Ashbourne Road with two of his sisters who had cared for him. However the sisters had both died by 1892 and perhaps William was on the lookout for someone else to look after him. Was William and Kitty's marriage one of convenience where he gained a replacement housekeeper and she married a comparatively wealthy man? After her marriage Kitty moved from a terraced house in a court to a finer house in Ashbourne Road. No 1, Brooklands was a considerably larger and more prestigious house than the house she had lived in with her family. In 1900, when the late William Goostrey's house was offered for sale, his house was described as a charming and desirable villa residence with lawns and gardens and included building land then used as pleasure grounds. William and Kitty died within a few months of each other in 1900. William left an estate valued at over £9,000 but perhaps he did not leave Kitty a great deal of money as when she died her estate, which she left to her brother, only amounted to £270.

Above
William and Kitty's home at no. 1 Brooklands in Ashbourne Road. The houses on the right were built on land which was once their pleasure gardens

The Redfern Cousins

The Redferns were a family of solicitors in Leek. Thomas Redfern (1801-1864) was a respected man whose practice was in Church Lane and who lived at Daisy Bank House. Daisy Bank was a large property whose grounds comprised both kitchen and pleasure gardens, including a vinery and a peach house, a coach house and stables. The Redfern family was comfortably off. Thomas had two sons, Thomas, junior, and John, who both became solicitors, both these sons had daughters who were pictured with Elizabeth Wardle in 1888. John Redfern's daughter, Annie, is featured in the Khartoum Frontal Chapter (see page 152).

Right
Thomas Redfern

Frances Christina Redfern
1872- 1949

Above
Cissie Redfern one of Elizabeth Wardle's embroidery pupils

Frances Christina, known as Cissie, was the daughter of Thomas Redfern, junior (1827-1898) and Francis Sophia Lightfoot. As a child she lived at Daisy Bank House with her parents. Thomas Redfern, junior, worked from his father's former premises in Church Lane and dealt with a great deal of business in the town. The Redfern family worshipped at St Edward's where Thomas was a churchwarden. He would seem to have been more affluent than his younger brother, John, who also practiced as a solicitor in Leek. However Thomas Redfern's family suffered a blow in 1886 when Thomas was taken into custody awaiting trial for fraud, he was found guilty and sentenced to four calendar months in the common gaol at Stafford and went bankrupt the same year. Anne Lowe who stitched for the Leek Embroidery Society recorded this event in her diary with dismay referring to Thomas' wife as "Poor Fanny". This reversal of fortune resulted in the family leaving Daisy Bank House to live in Queen Street. Although their house at 29b Queen Street was a fine town house, designed by Larner Sugden, it would have been a step down from the house and grounds at Daisy Bank where the family had been living.

Cissie was a pupil of Elizabeth Wardle but census returns show that she did not work as an embroiderer and never had a paid occupation of any kind. By the time her father died in 1898 the family were living in Westwood Road and in 1901 Cissie and her mother, Frances Sophia, are in lodgings in Llandudno. Whether they were living there or merely visiting is not known, but Francis is living on her own means and her 29 year old daughter, Cissie, does not work for her living. Frances Sophia Redfern (nee Lightfoot) had her own income from a trust fund set up for her as a marriage settlement when she married Thomas Redfern, junior, in 1868.The trust was for the sole benefit of Frances Sophia for her life and then for the benefit of the couple's children. This settlement would have enabled her to live comfortably after her husband died.

Above
Daisy Bank House, the house was once much larger having an additional storey

By 1911 Cissie and her mother are living in Bournemouth where a hospital nurse is employed to look after Francis Sophia who is now infirm. Francis Sophia died in Bournemouth in 1913 and Frances Christina in the Conway district.

The only known example of Frances Christina Redfern's work is the 'Four Kings' altar frontal for St Edward's Church which was stitched when she was one of Elizabeth Wardle's needlewomen.

Charlotte Louise Robinson
born 1876

Charlotte was a member of the Leek Embroidery Society and was contracted to work for them. An entry in St Edward's Parish magazine records that in 1895 "*The Embroidery Society has done much good work, but it will not easily surpass the King Frontal. I am told that the figures are the first which have been worked in Leek, and that King Ethelbert and a portion of King Edward have been elaborated by the skilful fingers of Miss Charlotte Robinson.*" The Four Kings Frontal had been presented to the church by Mrs Elizabeth Wardle in 1895. However, in 1896, an agreement was drawn up between Charlotte and the Embroidery Society which allowed Charlotte to be free to work 'for other than the Society'. She was allowed to do figure embroidery, designing and colouring of designs on paper, but she was emphatically not free to do embroidery recognized as 'Leek Embroidery' or Church work as done by the Society.

Charlotte then began to work half days for the Leek Embroidery Society and went into business on her own account. By the age of 25 she was the director of an art depot in Leek. In 1907 she advertised in the *Leek Times* informing customers that her shop at 10 St Edward Street would be opened on Saturday 24th August. She ran an art embroidery shop, as Charlotte Robinson & Co. from these premises until she moved to other premises in St Edward Street.

In July 1911, when Charlotte worked in Art embroidery, the properties at 10 and 12 St Edward Street were offered for sale at The Swan Hotel. The premises consisted of a leather curriers shop and an art embroidery shop occupied by Charlotte. Charlotte's premises comprised the shop, a workroom over the shop and 2 bedrooms on the second floor plus an attic bedroom, a box room and a scullery with a water tap in Booth's back yard. Charlotte Robinson ran the business from these premises for many years but by 1928 had moved further down the street to No. 40 where she remained in business until at least 1936.

Right
St Edward Street, Charlotte's shop at No 10 can be seen on the right with the roof windows

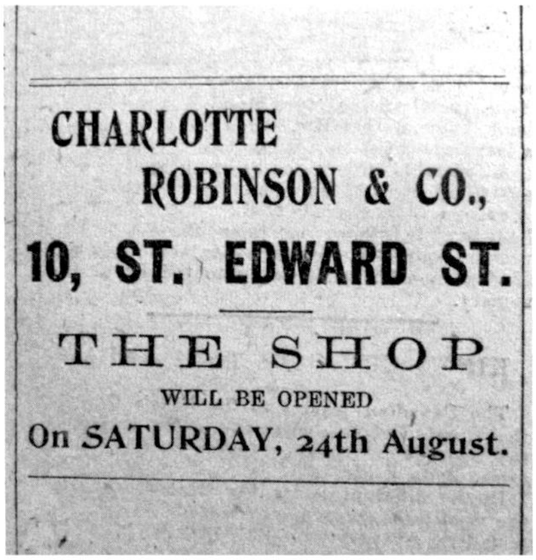

CHARLOTTE
ROBINSON & CO.,
10, ST. EDWARD ST.

THE SHOP
WILL BE OPENED
On SATURDAY, 24th August.

Below
Advert for Charlotte Robinson & Co. dated 1907

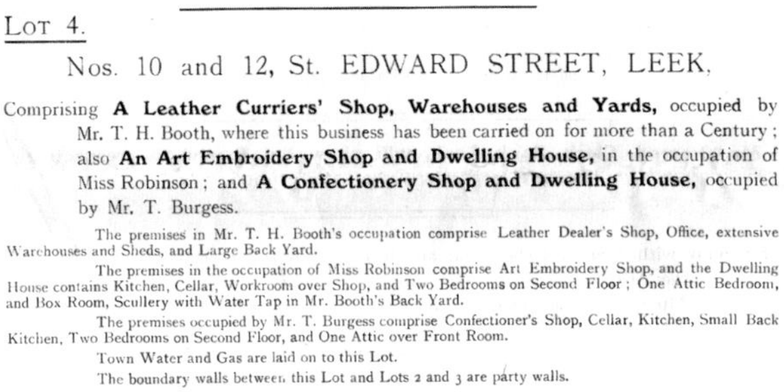

LOT 4.

Nos. 10 and 12, St. EDWARD STREET, LEEK.

Comprising **A Leather Curriers' Shop, Warehouses and Yards,** occupied by Mr. T. H. Booth, where this business has been carried on for more than a Century; also **An Art Embroidery Shop and Dwelling House,** in the occupation of Miss Robinson; and **A Confectionery Shop and Dwelling House,** occupied by Mr. T. Burgess.

The premises in Mr. T. H. Booth's occupation comprise Leather Dealer's Shop, Office, extensive Warehouses and Sheds, and Large Back Yard.

The premises in the occupation of Miss Robinson comprise Art Embroidery Shop, and the Dwelling House contains Kitchen, Cellar, Workroom over Shop, and Two Bedrooms on Second Floor; One Attic Bedroom, and Box Room, Scullery with Water Tap in Mr. Booth's Back Yard.

The premises occupied by Mr. T. Burgess comprise Confectioner's Shop, Cellar, Kitchen, Small Back Kitchen, Two Bedrooms on Second Floor, and One Attic over Front Room.

Town Water and Gas are laid on to this Lot.

The boundary walls between this Lot and Lots 2 and 3 are party walls.

Above
Sale notice for the premises in 1911

Right
Nab Hill House, the home of the Robinson family

Interestingly and indicative of the many connections between Leek families the property at 10 St Edward Street had once been owned by the Young family who were related to Elizabeth Wardle.

A young woman may have needed capital to set up a business and to rent premises and perhaps Charlotte was helped by her father, Thomas Robinson, who for many years was the managing clerk at Challinor and Shaw's solicitor's practice in Leek. Thomas and Elizabeth Wardle's son worked as a solicitor at Challinor & Shaw's. This firm of lawyers, who operated from the elegant Georgian house at 10 Derby Street, acted for Thomas Wardle. Thomas Robinson had many contacts in Leek as he was at one time a director of the Leek and Moorlands Building Society, an overseer of the poor, a member of Leek Urban District Council, the honorary secretary of the Leek Chamber of Commerce (silk section) and a staunch supporter of the Conservative Party. His fellow directors and councillors were, for the most part, silk manufacturers, doctors, and prominent businessmen whose wives and daughters would be potential purchasers of the needlework produced by Charlotte's company. The Robinson family lived at Nab Hill House in the West end of the town, a substantial detached property with extensive gardens. Charlotte's eldest brother, Colin, died in the Great War and is commemorated on the Nicholson War Memorial. Her brother, John, became a bank manager, her eldest sister, Mary, married a Leek tailor, her sister Elsie married a Manchester surgeon. Charlotte's youngest sister, Jean married a clergyman who became the vicar at Meerbrook. Charlotte was a spinster in 1911 and no records have been discovered to date recording a marriage or her death.

The Vigrass Sisters

Ellen Vigrass
1872 - 1941

Ethel Vigrass
1883 – 1974

The Vigrass sisters were both born at 13 York Street in Leek where they lived with their parents until the family moved to a larger house at 72 Westwood Road. Their father Charles Vigrass worked as a clerk to a silk manufacturer; their mother Selina, nee Ollerenshaw, had worked as the housekeeper for the Goodwin family at 47 St Edward Street before her marriage. This house is almost opposite 62 St Edward Street where Thomas and Elizabeth Wardle were living at the time. Stephen Goodwin was a silk manufacturer whose Britannia silk mill was situated at the corner of West Street and Salisbury Street.

Right
No 47 St Edward Street on the extreme left

Above
Nellie Vigrass

Right
Nellie when a young woman

Ellen Vigrass, known as Nellie, is pictured with Elizabeth Wardle in 1888 and was an embroidery pupil. However, although Ellen helped to stitch the 'Four Kings' altar frontal in St Edward's church in Leek, with other needlewomen, she did not go on to work as an embroiderer. Instead she moved away from Leek first working as a ladies maid in Surrey and then going into business as a partner in a boarding house in Kensington. She never married and returned to the family home at 72 Westwood Road where she died in 1941.

Right
Embroidery by Ethel Vigrass

WORKED BY MISS ETHEL VIGRASS,
A PUPIL OF LADY WARDLE'S
"SCHOOL OF EMBROIDERY FOR YOUNG LADIES."
CIRCA 1895.

Ethel Vigrass, who was a milliner by profession, remained in the family home in Westwood Road all her life. A finely stitched floral panel, worked by Ethel, can be seen in St Edward's church in Leek. The label on the framed embroidery states that Ethel was a member of the Embroidery Society. She was also a member of the Girls Friendly Society who worked the sanctuary carpet for the church.

Above
Ethel Vigrass

Above, top right
Ethel Vigrass in later years

Above, bottom right
Westwood Road

Sarah Young
1838- 1943

Sarah Young was Elizabeth Wardle's cousin, the daughter of Samuel Young and his wife Catherine. She is most probably the Miss Young who worked on the Khartoum frontal too. Sarah spent her childhood at Lyme House Farm in Longsdon before moving to Hugo Street in Leek with her widowed father in the 1880s. She stayed on in Hugo Street after her father had died and still lived there in 1891 with her niece, Helen Dilworth, who also stitched Leek Embroidery. Ten years later Sarah lived at Ross in Herefordshire where one of her visitors was her aunt, Ann Smith, another member of the Embroidery Society who stitched an Altar frontal for St Luke's church at Endon and part of the facsimile of the Bayeux Tapestry. Sarah Young's sister, Mary, was one of the women who stitched the Pelican frontal in 1872 and Jennie Smith, the wife of her cousin Charles, stitched a panel of the facsimile of the Bayeux Tapestry. Additionally Sarah's cousins Florence and Alice Pattinson also stitched panels of the facsimile of the Bayeux Tapestry. Another indication of the close family relationships often found between the women who stitched for the Leek Embroidery Society.
By 1921 Sarah Young, a woman of independent means, had moved to Edge Moor cottage at Verwood in Dorset where she died in 1933. Sarah's brother, Barnet Young, died in 1921 leaving £29,739 to Sarah.

Right
Litany fall stitched by Sarah Young for All Saints Church in Leek

Right
Lyme House

The Khartoum Frontal

A letter, written by Edward Challinor in 1905, informed interested parties that an altar cloth, which had been worked by several Leek ladies, would be on view at the Leek Embroidery Society. He was referring to the altar cloth or frontal which was to be presented to the English Church at Khartoum, which was still under construction at that time. Edward Challinor was hoping that further contributions towards the cost of the frontal would be received. Anyone interested in viewing the frontal would find it in the Embroidery Society's premises at 56 St Edward Street, next door to the Wardle's town house. Lydia Wardle, daughter of Thomas and Elizabeth, would be collecting the contributions. Lydia had been running the Leek Embroidery Society since the death of her mother in 1902. The altar cloth was finished by April 1905 although the church in Khartoum was not yet completed.

Background Image
Detail form an altar frontal at St Luke's church in Endon which is the sane design and colour as the one stitched for Khartoum

Above
An altar frontal at St Luke's church in Endon which is the sane design and colour as the one stitched for Khartoum

Edward Challinor is described as the originator {sic} of the altar frontal and the name 'Challinor' is by far the predominate name in the list of women who worked this frontal. The connection between the Challinor family and Khartoum is explained by the name of the woman at the head of the list. She is Mrs Phipps who, before her marriage, was Jessica Mabel Challinor and was Edward's sister. Her husband Constantine Osbourne Phipps had a brother named Pownoll Ramsey Phipps. Pownoll was a military man, a Major in 1905, who was serving in the Sudan and who was the honorary secretary of the Khartoum Cathedral Fund until 1912. Additionally Pownoll Phipps was the private secretary of Sudan's governor general, Sir Reginald Wingate, as well as his close friend. Letters from Wingate's wife, Lady Kitty Wingate, regarding the safe arrival of the frontal in Khartoum can be found in the local studies archive at Leek Public Library. Edward Challinor was a close family friend of the Wardle's and was the godfather of Joan Underhill, the daughter of Walter and Edith Underhill (nee Wardle).

A Miss Fowler also stitched this frontal but has not yet been positively identified.

Right
Details from the super frontal stitched for Khartoum

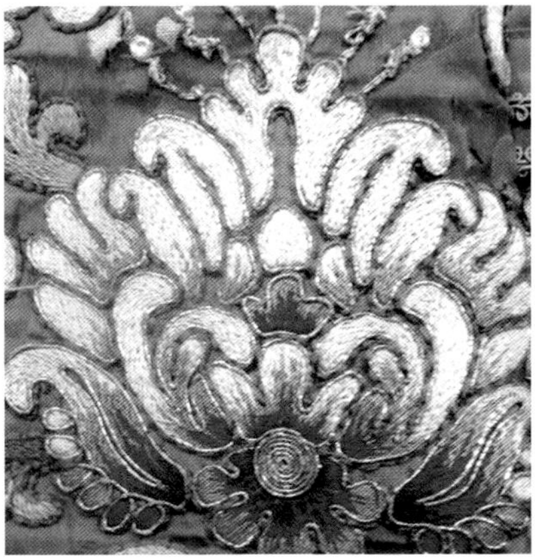

Right
Letter from Edward Challinor

The Park,

Leek,

27th January, 1905.

Dear

On Monday next the 30th, till the following Saturday, an Altar Cloth worked by Ladies of Leek will be on view at the Leek Embroidery Society between 10-30 and 12-30, and 2 and 4 o'clock. The Cloth is to be presented to the English Church at Khartoum which is now being built to the memory of the late General Gordon. Contributions towards the Cloth will be gratefully received by Miss Wardle, St. Edward Street.

Yours truly,

E. CHALLINOR.

The Allen sisters

Below
The Wardle family lived in the house in the centre of this photograph, the bay window of the embroidery shop can be seen below. Above the Wardle house is the home and offices of William Allen

Catherine, Alice and Eliza were daughters of William and Eliza Allen. Their father, a Leek solicitor, was a very busy man who played a prominent role in the life of the town. During his life he had been a church warden at St Edward's Church, president of Leek Cricket Club, a trustee of the Ancient Order of Foresters and a patron of Leek Amateur Musical Society. In his professional life he was a senior partner in the firm of Hacker and Allen whose offices were at 52 St Edward Street next door to Thomas and Elizabeth Wardle's town house. William Allen was the registrar and high bailiff of the county court and law clerk to the Leek Improvement Commissioners and to the later Urban District Council. The Allen family home was at 50 St Edward Street. When William Allen died his obituary in local newspapers referred to him as 'Leek's grand old man'.

Catherine Mary Allen (later Challinor)
1856 – 1950

The Allen sisters were all members of the Leek branch of the Primrose League and sang with the Leek Amateur Musical Society. Catherine was one of that society's principal vocalists in 1887. She is remembered by her family as a good pianist and a sweet singer, excellent attributes for a young lady in Victorian days. She was a petite woman who also had a short temper and could be jealous of her sisters. Educated in France she was a life long Francophile, indulged by her husband she stayed each year in Menton in France for a month. This allowed her younger sister, Alice, to descend on Catherine's home at Pickwood Hall to organize a severe spring cleaning! Throughout her life Catherine was deeply religious and undertook charity work in aid of St Luke's church where she worshipped after her marriage to William Edward Challinor, an earthenware manufacturer. William and Catherine lived at Haregate Hall and later at 62 St Edward Street, which was Thomas and Elizabeth Wardle's home when the Wardle's first moved to Leek. After the death of her father-in-law Catherine and her family moved into Pickwood Hall, the Challinor family's home on the outskirts of Leek. William Edward Challinor died in 1926 at Pickwood but Catherine outlived her husband dying, in 1950, at the home of friends in Buxton with whom she had been residing for the past four years. Her obituary makes reference to her well known work for charity; she was on the committee of the Leek Charity Organization Society for many years, and had also been president of both the Cruso Nursing Association and St Luke's Mothers Union. Catherine helped to stitch the Khartoum Frontal in 1905 as did her daughters Kathleen and Elizabeth Challinor. At the time Catherine and her family were all members of the congregation at St Luke's Church.

Above
No. 50 and 52 St Edward Street, the Allen family home and offices being converted into building society offices.

Right
The former Allen home still in use as the headquarters of a local building society

Alice Allen
1862 – 1948

Alice Allen never married and lived for most of her life at the Allen family home in St Edward Street. She left her family home after 1916 when it was converted into new premises for the Leek United Permanent Benefit Building Society and moved to a large house in Moorfields with an unmarried sister. Later the sisters moved to Buxton where they lived until their deaths. Alice was regarded as the beauty of the family, a prolific needlewoman who stitched handkerchief cases, tray cloths and pin cushions which she regularly presented to her nieces. With her sisters she took part in both amateur dramatics and in performances by the Leek Amateur Musical Society at the Temperance Hall in Union Street. In 1882 the Allen sisters sang 'The Venetian Boat Song' at a concert there. She also sang in amateur concerts in aid of St Luke's church and in 1900 took part in a 'Grand Dramatic Performance' in Leek Town Hall in aid of the Soldiers and Sailors Families Association whose president at the time was Lady Wardle.
Besides helping with the Khartoum Frontal Alice also embroidered panel 10 of the facsimile of the Bayeux Tapestry and in 1934 stitched another facsimile panel which depicts the funeral of Edward. This panel is in the Staffordshire Moorlands District Council's archive.

Above
Bayeux Tapestry
panel stitched by
Alice Allen in 1934

Staffordshire
Moorlands District
Council Archive

Eliza (Lizzie) Allen
1864- 1949

Although Lizzie did not contribute to the embroidery on the Khartoum Frontal it seems appropriate to include her here with her sisters.
Eliza lived at 50 St Edward Street with her parents and siblings until 1889 when she married Thomas Sandby Coombe, a physician and surgeon. They moved to Purton, a village in Wiltshire, where they employed a governess to teach their daughter. The family lived in Purton until at least 1909 before moving to Cranham, a village in Gloucestershire, just twenty miles away. Thomas and Eliza moved again this time to Hoo St Werburgh in Kent where Thomas worked as a medical officer at the Hoo Rural District Hospital for Infectious Diseases. By 1917 they had settled in Folkestone where they received news that their eighteen year old only son Allen Sandby, a probationary flight officer, had lost his life.

Below
Phoenix on the superfrontal in St Edward's Church in Leek

Above
Ladies at Pickwood Hall

Before her marriage Lizzie traced the cartoons, which had been borrowed from the South Kensington Museum, so that the embroiderers could faithfully reproduce their facsimile of the Bayeux Tapestry. She is reputed to have designed the Phoenix on the superfrontal of the white altar frontal in Leek's St Edward's church. Lizzie Coombe was one of the designers whose work was shown at the silk exhibition held in the Lecture Room at The Nicholson Institute in Leek when the new Municipal Technical and High School and County Silk School was opened by Her Royal Highness Princess Victoria May, Duchess of York, in July 1900.

Clara Bill (nee Troost)
1870-1954

Clara Amelia Auguste Troost was born in Saxony, the name of her father is not known but her mother was Freida Troost. Freida was born in Germany, about 1846, and died in St Edward Street in Leek in 1913. Clara and her mother were living in Leek by 1891 when Clara worked as a silk warehousewoman. That year an advertisement was placed in the Leek Times by a German woman offering to give lessons in "her own language".
In 1897 an agreement was made between Clara Troost and Lady Wardle (for the Leek Embroidery Society), this was a legal contract stipulating the terms under which Clara would be employed. It is only one of two such agreements that have yet been discovered and confirms that Elizabeth Wardle was running a tightly controlled business. Miss Troost had to agree not to do any work for sale which touched on embroidery or on making up either with Leek embroidery designs or any other designs. She was not to teach or to give advice on embroidery or on making up so long as she continued on the staff of the Leek Embroidery Society. The society in return agreed to find her employment for five and a half days a week, consisting of forty six hours, for which she would be paid 17/6d per week. If necessary the society would also provide homework in addition up to another 7/6d per week. If anyone were to ask Clara Troost for embroidery lessons or to stitch or make up pieces they were to be referred to the Leek Embroidery Society at once.
The society agreed that Clara could take orders for white linen work, embossing handkerchiefs, plain sewing, bead work, knitting crochet, lacework, or anything else to be done at home which did not touch in the least on embroidery or making up. Freida Troost, Clara's mother, also had to undertake not to touch on these points, either in advising any person, giving lessons to any person, on working or making up anything for sale for any person so long as her daughter is on the staff of the Leek Embroidery Society.

Above
The Leek Embroidery Society shop moved to the other side of St Edward Street and can be seen here in the left foreground

Freida Troost was employed for a while as a housekeeper by Frederic Simoni at 18 Deansgate in Leek. Frederic was of Italian descent and had a music shop at 23 St Edward Street where he sold all kinds of musical instruments including American organs, harmoniums and concertinas. He was also a talented violinist playing in local amateur musical societies. Perhaps he influenced Clara to take part in amateur entertainment as a report in the *Leek Times* in 1900 records that Clara sang 'Riding on a Load of Hay' at a Popular Concert.

Right
Banner at St Peter's church in Stoke stitched by Clara Bill and Lydia Wardle.
He Hath Broken the Gates of Brass

Right
Madonna and Child panel in St Edward's Church at Cheddleton, stitched by Clara Bill

In 1901, shortly before her marriage to Arthur Bill, Clara and Freida lived in Russell Street in Leek. Freida no longer worked but Clara was employed as a fancy textile embroiderer.
Arthur Bill had his own business working as a carriage and general smith. In 1911 Clara and Arthur lived in Derby Street, Clara states on that census return that she worked for an Embroidery School as a hand embroideress [sic]. The terms Leek Embroidery Society and Leek Embroidery School both existed at this time as in 1908 Bessie Brunt is recorded as secretary of both the Leek Embroidery Society and of the Leek School of Embroidery.
After Elizabeth Wardle died, in 1902, Clara ran the Leek Embroidery Society with Lydia Wardle. The business still operated from 54 St Edward Street for many years until Clara took the shop across the road to no 21. A descendent of one of the needlewomen can remember going to this shop with her Aunt when a very young child. She sat on a chair in the shop while her aunt consulted with Clara Bill about which silks she needed to purchase for a particular piece of embroidery. In 1930 Clara sold the shop to Mrs Annie Sutton who with Miss Marrett ran an Art Needlework Depot there.
Evidence from descendants of Clara Bill's friends indicates that during WWII she lived in the village of Cheddleton. In the 1940s St Edward's Church at Cheddleton purchased a frontal, designed by Edmund Street, which Clara altered. Her husband made a frame for the frontal.
In addition to stitching the altar frontal for Khartoum Clara worked a picture of the Madonna and Child, which can be seen in the Lady Chapel at St Edward the Confessor in Cheddleton. She also helped to stitch a banner 'He hath broken the gates of brass' for Stoke Parish Church. Clara was the needlewoman who joined together the panels of the facsimile of the Bayeux Tapestry. She died at Lower House Farm in Rainow, near Macclesfield.

Right
Leek Embroidery Society Advertisement

LEEK EMBROIDERY SOCIETY
ESTABLISHED BY THE LATE LADY WARDLE, 1880.
21, ST. EDWARD STREET, LEEK.

Church Work a Speciality. Artistic and White Linen Embroidery of every kind supplied and Jumper Wools
MATERIALS PROVIDED.

Right
Leek Embroidery Society Contract

LEEK EMBROIDERY SOCIETY

ADDRESS:
Leek Embroidery Society,
St. Edward Street,
LEEK, STAFFS.,
May 31 1897

Miss Frost to do absolutely no work for sale, of any kind whatever, which touches on embroidery, or on making-up: either with our designs or with any other designs: for any person whatsoever; and she is not to teach, or give advice upon, either of these branches, so long

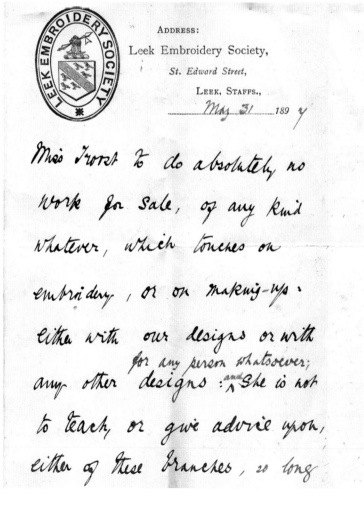

Janie Challinor nee Ellis
1862-1940

The Mrs E Challinor who is listed as one of the needlewoman who stitched the Khartoum Frontal is Janie Ellis. Janie was the daughter of Lilley Ellis (a male) who had been a silk merchant in Leek for the firm of Ellis, Russell and Clowes, which was situated on the corner of Salisbury Street and West Street. (This mill was later occupied by the silk firm of Stephen Goodwin and Tatton). In 1854 Lilley Ellis left Leek and started a business of ship dyers, cleaners and furnishers in Birkenhead living just a few miles away in Rock Ferry. Janie Ellis, who was born in Rock Ferry, married Edward Challinor at St Paul's Church in Tranmere in 1886. The couple settled at 'The Park' one of the semi-detached Park Villas built on the Ball Haye estate. Edward Challinor, a Leek solicitor, was the 'originator' [sic] of the Khartoum frontal so it

Right
The Park, on the right of this photograph, once the home of Edward Challinor

Above
The Challinor Fountain
In 1876 Mary Edith Challinor (later Watson) unveiled the fountain presented to the town by her father, William. The fountain stood in the Market Place but now stands in front of Moorland House in Stockwell Street

is not surprising that several of his relatives worked on the frontal. Edward Challinor died in 1908 at the relatively young age of forty four. His wife, who now had 'private means' moved with her daughters to 10 Stockwell Street in Leek, a Georgian house which still stands. Here Janie had a domestic servant and a governess for her youngest daughter. Later Janie Challinor returned to her roots dying in the Birkenhead district in 1940.

L Ellis

This mysterious girl was also one of the women who stitched the Khartoum Altar Frontal. She is listed with other unmarried young women who worked this piece. However research has not been able to identify a Miss L Ellis. Nevertheless there is a strong link with an Ellis family who lived in Leek and I suggest that this elusive young lady is Miss F Ellis.

Right
Knivedon Hall once the home of the Ellis family

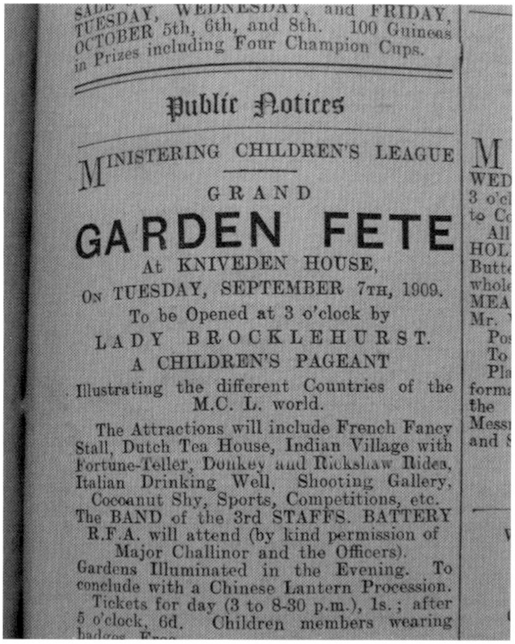
TUESDAY, WEDNESDAY, and FRIDAY, OCTOBER 5th, 6th, and 8th. 100 Guineas in Prizes including Four Champion Cups.

Public Notices

MINISTERING CHILDREN'S LEAGUE

GRAND

GARDEN FETE

At KNIVEDEN HOUSE,

On TUESDAY, SEPTEMBER 7TH, 1909.

To be Opened at 3 o'clock by

LADY BROCKLEHURST.

A CHILDREN'S PAGEANT

Illustrating the different Countries of the M.C. L. world.

The Attractions will include French Fancy Stall, Dutch Tea House, Indian Village with Fortune-Teller, Donkey and Rickshaw Rides, Italian Drinking Well, Shooting Gallery, Cocoanut Shy, Sports, Competitions, etc.

The BAND of the 3rd STAFFS. BATTERY R.F.A. will attend (by kind permission of Major Challinor and the Officers).

Gardens Illuminated in the Evening. To conclude with a Chinese Lantern Procession.

Tickets for day (3 to 8-30 p.m.), 1s.; after 5 o'clock, 6d. Children members wearing

Right
A notice informing the public of a Garden Fête at Knivedon House in 1909

Janie Ellis (see pages 136-137) had an elder sister named Florence who married Clement Campbell Ellis, an East India merchant, in Calcutta. Florence's elder children were born in Bengal and Burma but others were born after the family returned to England in the 1890s. They settled in Lancaster Gate in London where they had a staff of nine servants. In 1902, Clement Ellis purchased the Knivedon estate on Mount Road in Leek. *Leek Annuals* record Knivedon as the home of the Ellis family from 1904. Clement Ellis's widow still lived there in 1921 after the death of her husband. Their eldest daughter, Florence Bertha who was born in 1887, married William Francis Challinor in Leek in 1917. He was related to her aunt's husband, Edward Challinor. I would put forward Florence Bertha Ellis as the unidentified needlewoman who helped to stitch the Khartoum frontal. A letter in the local history archive at Leek Library records that Clement Ellis, Florence's father, had offered to arrange for the delivery of the frontal to Khartoum free of charge.

Jessie Mabel Phipps nee Challinor
1864- 1926

Jessie, often known as Mabel, was the daughter of Joseph Challinor, a solicitor, who lived at Compton House in Leek. Joseph employed twenty two clerks at his offices in Derby Street. A photograph of the smartly dressed Challinor family in their pony and trap is indicative of the status of the family who led a somewhat privileged life style compared to most Leek residents. Jessie attended the Mechanics Institute Art Classes where she was awarded a prize for "monochrome painting of ornament from the copy" and gained a certificate for model drawing.

In 1886 she married the Reverend Canon Constantine Osbourne Phipps at St Edward's Church in Leek where the service was conducted by the vicars of both St Edward's and All Saints Churches. Constantine Phipps father's diary records that he stayed at Foxlowe with Mrs Cruso whom he described as a very nice and rich old lady!

The report of Jessie's marriage in local newspapers reads like a who's who of Leek's middle class, although one paper was keen to point out that many members of the working class attended the marriage as they were so fond of the Challinor family. The strong link between the Challinor and Wardle families is apparent as many members of the Wardle family were guests at the wedding and gave gifts to the happy couple. It is interesting to speculate that the fire screen, chair backs, and afternoon tea cloth given by Thomas and Elizabeth Wardle's daughters were possibly items of Leek embroidery which they had personally stitched. It is known that members of the Leek Embroidery Society did give hand embroidered gifts as wedding presents. Indeed Jessie Challinor had given her sister Leek Embroidery as a wedding gift. Many women who stitched Leek Embroidery were guests at Jessie's wedding including Marianne Nicholson, Lucy Pidcock, Margaret Ritchie, Alice Allen and the Misses Young.

Above
Compton House

Above
Joseph Challinor on horseback outside Compton House

Above
Joseph Challinor, Jessie's father

In common with other wives of clergymen Jessie lived in several vicarages as her husband was transferred from parish to parish. They lived at Cookham and in Aylsbury before moving, in 1914, to St John the Baptist, The Lee, Buckinghamshire. This last church has a processional cross in memory of Jessie Phipps. While they lived in Aylesbury, Jessie and her husband hosted a garden party in the grounds of the vicarage in aid of the local Temperance Society. She was involved with both the Mother's Union and the local Girls Friendly Society and she often presented prizes at events. Doubtless she and her husband attended a public dance in the Town Hall at Aylesbury in 1907 as her husband was one of the patrons as were members of the Rothschild banking family. The dance was held to raise money for the Royal Bucks Hospital and the Royal Agricultural Benevolent Institution. As her husband was also President of the Vale of Aylesbury Sacred Harmonic Society she would have accompanied him to concerts staged by that society in the Corn Exchange and other venues.
As a married woman Jessie had helped to stitch the Khartoum Frontal and before her marriage she had stitched panel 3 of the Bayeux Tapestry. She died in Aylesbury in 1926.

Constantine and Jessie had two daughters and two sons, tragically both sons were killed in WWI. Evelyn Phipps, one of Jessie's daughters, married Ivor Stewart in 1913. Ivor was the nephew of Arthur Lasenby Liberty the founder of the famous Liberty store in London. Ivor added the Liberty name to his surname and as Ivor Stewart Liberty inherited the Liberty business and was chairman of Liberty & Co. Ltd until his death in 1952.

Below
The Challinor family leaving Compton House for an outing

How interesting that a member of Leek Embroidery Society, who stitched Tussur silk dyed by Thomas Wardle, who dyed silk for Liberty's, became the mother-in-law of the head of the famous Liberty store. The Challinor family forged another link with the Wardle's when Jessie's sister, Mary Blanche Challinor, married Gilbert Wardle in 1893. Gilbert was the son of Thomas and Elizabeth Wardle.

Helen (Nellie) Challinor
1867 – 1938

Below
Former home and offices of the Challinor family in Derby Street, Leek

Helen Challinor was the sister of Jessie Phipps nee Challinor. Helen Challinor is with her sister, Mary Blanche, in Torquay in 1891. They are travelling with Frances Gailey another Leek embroiderer. Helen grew up at Compton House in Leek, she did not marry and died in Leek in 1938.

The Fearon Sisters

Mary Fearon
b. 1878

Katherine Fearon
1880-1920

Katherine and Mary were born at Norton-in-the-Moors, a village near Leek, where their father was the rector. Their father later became the vicar at St Edward's Church in Leek and the sisters were living with their parents in the vicarage, next to the church, when they helped to stitch the Khartoum Altar Frontal in 1905. Katherine was an accomplished violinist and pianist and took a keen interest in amateur entertainment in Leek often playing for the Leek Orchestral Society. As the daughters of a clergyman Katherine and Mary would have taken part in both ecclesiastical and secular activities and would have come into close contact with the Wardle family, who worshipped at St Edward's church. While their father was the vicar of St Edward's Thomas Wardle was striving to ensure that the new Condylffe stained glass window and the rose windows in the church were of the best design. Thomas Wardle became Katherine Fearon's father-in-law when she married his son, Gilbert, in 1906. She was Gilbert Wardle's second wife as his first wife, Mary Blanche Challinor, had died in 1901. Katherine and Gilbert lived at Southfields after their marriage before moving to 54 St Edward Street where they employed four domestic servants. Some years later they moved to Compton House which had been the home of his first wife. Katherine died at Compton house when only forty years old leaving her husband with six young children.

The originator [sic] of the Khartoum Frontal was Edward Challinor the brother of Gilbert Wardle's first wife. Yet another indication of the close family links which existed in many ways between the women who stitched for the Leek Embroidery Society.

Above
St Edward's Church in Leek

Above, right
St Edward's Vicarage where the Fearon sisters lived with their parents

Right
Gilbert Wardle, Katherine's husband

After Thomas Fearon's death in 1904 his widow and daughters left Leek to set up home in the village of Otterbourne in Hampshire. Mary Fearon spent the remainder of her life there living with her widowed mother and a younger sister.

Kate Hall
1878 – 1953

Opposite Page: Top, left
Ball Haye Hall

Opposite Page: Top, right
Heath Cross, Cheddelton Heath

Opposite Page: Bottom
Former Lake in the grounds of Ball Haye Hall, now the duck pond in the park

Kate Hall was the daughter of John and Sarah Hall and lived for most of her life in Ball Haye Hall, a substantial property, now demolished, which stood near to the present day swimming baths in Leek. Her father was a silk manufacturer, a partner at Brough, Nicholson & Hall whose leading products included the manufacture of sewing silks. The firm's extensive premises covered a large area and comprised several mills where upwards of 1,000 people were employed. John Hall was a wealthy man so Kate grew up in a household where a cook provided the meals and housemaids, kitchen maids and laundry maids looked after the family. Gardeners had their separate cottages on the estate and the coachman lived in the lodge on Ball Haye Green, which still survives. Kate would have spent summer days at the family's country retreat, Argyll Cottage, situated a few miles from Leek, near to Hen Cloud on the Roaches. Later renamed Roaches House, the property still stands and now caters for holidaymakers. The Hall children were privately educated, two of Kate's brothers were boarders at the Leys School in Cambridge, her younger brother was a boarder at Rydall Mount School in Wales and her sisters were educated at a ladies school in Cheltenham. It is not known if Kate was also educated privately.

Kate's father was a leading Wesleyan Methodist, a trustee of West Street Sunday School and a manager of Leek Council School as well as a J.P. No doubt Kate was in attendance when her father gave an address to the Duke and Duchess of York when they opened the Leek Municipal Technical and High School and County Silk School in 1900. John Hall was a generous man and would open the gardens at Ball Haye Hall on summer Sunday's for Leek people to enjoy. In 1929 Kate and her sister were present at the Annual Garden Party at Ball Haye when 300 people were invited to attend. On another occasion she supported her father at a charity event in the grounds on behalf of Wesleyan missionary work. The Salvation Army provided musical entertainment and games and

Above
John Hall reads an address at the opening of the Technical School in 1900

sports took place including an American Tennis Tournament. The Hall family also entertained teachers and scholars at their summer residence in the Roaches.

Kate Hall was a competent horsewoman and often rode out on her horse 'Satan', who was stabled with other horses at Ball Haye Hall.

After her father died Kate went to live at a newly built house on Cheddleton Heath named Heath Cross. She helped her eldest brother, John Howe Hall, to raise money for the planned new hospital for Leek which was to be built in the grounds of Ball Haye Hall. By 1938, £29,000 had been raised towards this project and members of the Hall family are still disappointed that this money was swallowed up by the National Health Service and that the new hospital for Leek never materialized.

Right
Kate Hall accompanied by her groom sets out for a ride on her horse 'Satan'

Kate appears to be the only member of the Hall family to remain in the Leek area, her brothers who had all been wealthy silk manufactures retired to the south coast to enjoy sunnier climes after they retired.

Kate Hall did not marry and died in a nursing home in Penkhull aged 75, she was a comparatively wealthy woman leaving an estate valued at £598,150.54.

Annie Millington Redfern
1875 -1953

Above
Annie Redfern

Annie Redfern was one of eight children born to John Redfern and his wife Emily. She was given the middle name of Millington as it was her grandmother's surname. Annie's father, John, was the son of Thomas Redfern and brother to Thomas Redfern, junior, while her mother was the daughter of John Lovatt, a silk manufacturer. Annie was a pupil of Elizabeth Wardle and stitched Leek embroidery all her life. She worked for the Embroidery Society and would have been one of the women who stitched items for sale in the shop in St Edward Street as well as working on church embroideries and exhibition pieces. Census returns from 1891 to 1911 show her occupation over the years as a fancy embroidery worker and a silk embroideress [sic]. On the 1911 census return Annie stated that she worked for a business concerned with "church and other embroidery."

Annie lived from an early age at 3 Cromwell Terrace in Leek, a terraced property which today overlooks Leek's bus station.

After her parents died Annie continued to live in Cromwell Terrace with her bachelor brother 'Charles' and her sister Emily. Charles was employed as a builder's clerk and Emily as a certified schoolmistress at the Leek Parish Church Schools in Mill Street. Annie's eldest brother was a patient for over 30 years at St Edward's Mental Hospital at Cheddleton. The politically incorrect census returns of that time describe him as a lunatic. All of John and Emily Redfern's children worked for their livings, not for them the life lived by their more affluent cousins (see page 107). Annie Redfern died at 3 Cromwell Terrace in 1953.

As well as helping to stitch the Khartoum Altar Frontal she embroidered a beautiful exhibition piece 'Adjanta', which is now part of Staffordshire Moorlands District Council's archive. This beautiful design is based on ancient cave paintings in India.

Right
Adjanta Panel
stitched by Annie
Redfern

Staffordshire
Moorlands District
Council Archive

Mary Elizabeth Turnock
1858-1929

Mary was one of the four daughters of Richard Turnock and Ruth Weston. Her father was a surgeon and general practitioner who lived and worked at 30 St Edward Street in Leek where Mary was born. Her mother was the daughter of John Weston who was a silk and button manufacturer. He owned land in Weston Street in Leek where he built houses including the villas which later became known as Roche View and Holmfield. The villas which were substantial properties with stables and gardens in the grounds were inherited by the Turnock sisters when their mother died.
Richard Turnock, Mary's father, may also have been involved in the silk industry as in 1869 he purchased "all that large building or silk factory now or lately used as a warehouse situated in a yard leading out of St Edward Street called the Globe Yard". This warehouse was very near to where the Turnock's lived in St Edward Street and of course the Turnocks were near neighbours of Thomas and Elizabeth Wardle. Doctor's enjoyed a high social status in Victorian days and as a doctor's daughter Elizabeth would have taken part in many social activities in the town. Her elder sisters, Margaret and Ann attended a private school in Leigh in Lancashire where the staff included a principle, two governesses and an assistant. Mary and her younger sister, Emily, do not appear to have been sent away to school but they did attend the Leek Art Classes. After Richard Turnock died, in 1875, his wife and daughters continued to live at 30 St Edward Street until their mother died in 1893. After their mother's death Mary Turnock and her elder sister, Margaret moved to Roche View, a large property in Weston Street, which had been built by their grandfather John Weston. The house in St Edward Street was rented for a period of seven years to a Miss Chambre (see Patience Gater text). The other Villa now named Holmfield eventually became the home of Mary's sister, Emily, who had moved away from Leek when she had married. In 1923, when Mary and Emily were elderly ladies, they were guests at the wedding of Lance

Above
Salter & Salters's shoe shop at the extreme left of the photograph was situated at no 32 St Edward Street. The Turnock family lived at no 30

Worthington at St Edward's church in Leek. It would seem that they still had a connection with the Wardle family as Lance Worthington was the son of Margaret Wardle and grandson of Thomas and Elizabeth Wardle.

Mary Elizabeth Turnock died at Roche View in 1929; her obituary in the *Leek Post* describes her as a member of a highly respected old Leek family who had been an active worker for St Edward's Church throughout her life. She was said to be 'of a quiet disposition and sincere in all her work'. Mary's funeral was attended by members of the Wardle family from Leekbrook.

Above
Roche View

J Unwin

Although a J Unwin is listed as one of the women who stitched the Khartoum frontal, no one of that name appears to live in Leek at this time. All of the other needlewomen, who stitched the Khartoum frontal, are from Leek or Leekbrook and are connected either to the Wardle family by blood or trade or are members of the Challinor family. So it would follow that J Unwin would also fit these criteria. There was an Unwin family who lived at 2 Church Street in Leek who were friends of Thomas and Elizabeth Wardle. Samuel Unwin was a solicitor and would also have known the solicitors in the Challinor family. In fact when Samuel Unwin's daughter, Mary Elizabeth, married Thomas W Atkinson in 1901 at St Edward's Church in Leek two of the wedding guests were Sir Thomas and Lady Wardle. Their gift to the bride and groom was a Leek embroidered tea cosy, clearly considered a valuable item. Another wedding gift was a carved oak corner cupboard given by Miss K Lowe. Katy Lowe was Thomas Wardle's secretary and is known to have made fine copper and wood carvings. Obviously Mary Elizabeth Unwin did not stitch the Khartoum frontal, as she was married by 1905, however she did have an elder sister named Constance, who never married and could have been the elusive needlewoman. Constance may be the Miss Unwin who worked on the communicant's kneeler for St Edward's church, in Leek, in 1907 as an associate of Girls Friendly Society. Some of the other women who worked on the kneeler are known to have been members of the Leek Embroidery Society.

Constance was born in 1870 and died, a spinster, in Buxton in 1949.

Above
2 Church Street
once the home of
the Unwin family

The Ward Connection

Frances Ann Gailey (nee Ward)
1851-1922

Frances is connected to several important families in Leek as her father John Ward was a partner in the firm of Anthony Ward & Sons who operated Albion Mill, the oldest silk mill in Leek. Her grandparents were Anthony Ward and Frances Ann Clover. The Clover family, who were wealthy shipbuilders in Birkenhead, also married into the Worthington family whose silk mills stood in Queen Street and Portland Street in Leek. Her nephew John Ward married into the influential Challinor family of solicitors in Leek. Frances spent her childhood at Southbank House which was situated quite close to the family silk mills in Albion Street. Frances' parents both died at this substantial house which later became the Southbank Hotel. The property was demolished some years ago and new housing now occupies the site.

Right
Albion Mill

Right
Ford House,
Stockwell Street

Frances Ann Ward married local doctor John Alexander Gailey in 1888. They lived at Ford House on the corner of Stockwell Street and Market Street. In 1891 Frances was on holiday in Torquay with Mary Blanche and Helen Challinor perhaps acting as their chaperone. Mary Blanche and Helen were also members of the Leek Embroidery Society. John Gailey died only four years after his marriage to Frances so the newly widowed Frances moved back to Southbank House to look after her elderly mother. After her mother died she moved to 4, Southfields where she employed two domestic servants. During her lifetime Frances was actively involved with the local community helping with the Mother's Union, the Boy Scout Movement, local schools and the Cottage Hospital. As a member of the Leek Embroidery Society she helped to stitch the Khartoum Altar Frontal in 1905.
Frances Gailey's funeral service was attended by members of the Wardle family from both Leek and Leekbrook. Margaret Wilson, whose first husband was Ernest Worthington, and Mary E Turnock also attended, all of these mourners had stitched embroidery for the Leek Embroidery Society.

Right
Anthony Ward & Co
Traveller's card

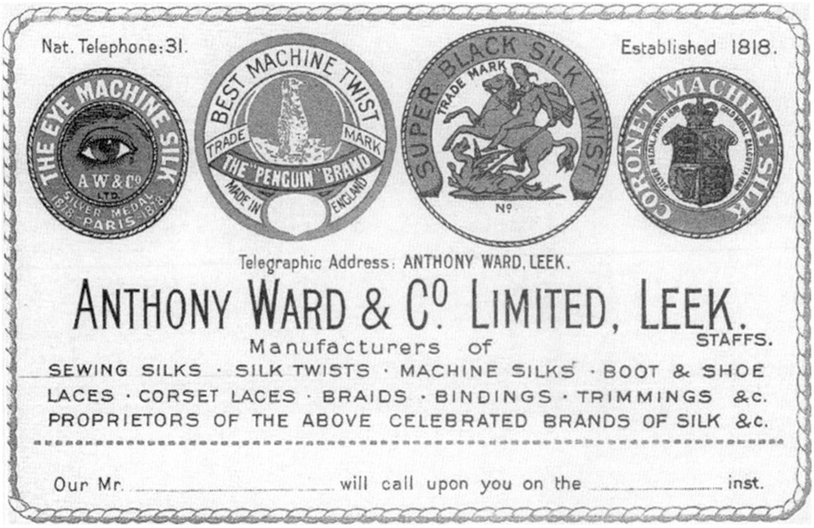

Right
John Ward, father of
Frances Ann Gailey

Mabel Ward
1882 – 1943

Mabel Ward was Frances Gailey's niece, the daughter of her brother Anthony. Mabel was also one of the needlewomen who stitched the Khartoum Frontal. She spent most of her childhood at Daisy Bank House but after the death of her grandmother in 1902 she moved into Southbank House with her parents. Mabel died a spinster in 1943 at the Cheadle Royal Hospital. Her obituary reveals that she had been an invalid for several years before her death.

Muriel Watson
1878-1973

Muriel was the daughter of Leek silk manufacturer William Saddington Watson and his wife Margaret, nee Russell. Her mother was one of the women who stitched the facsimile of the Bayeux Tapestry and is featured in that chapter. Muriel was born while the family lived in Horton Street when her father employed 143 hands at his silk mill in London Street and a cook, housemaid and nurse at his home. The Watson family moved to Lowe Hill House on the outskirts of Leek near to pleasant countryside, where they also employed several servants. Lowe Hill House, which still stands, is a large property which had twelve rooms in 1911.

In 1905 Muriel married local doctor Edgar Somerville at St Edward's Church in Leek. Edgar practiced from their home at 47 St Edward Street which in earlier years was the home of the Worthington sisters who stitched the Pelican frontal. Muriel and Edgar Somerville moved to Newton Abbott in Devon where they both died. Their daughter Margaret Helen Somerville lived to be a hundred, dying in Newton Abbott in 2006.

The Wardle Family

Background Image
Thomas Wardle with his children

Elizabeth Wardle
1834-1902

Elizabeth was the daughter of Hugh and Elizabeth Wardle, her father was a chemist and druggist. Both Elizabeth's parents came from affluent families. Her father, Hugh Wardle, was born at Rushton Spencer, a village near Leek on the road to Macclesfield. Hugh's father was James Wardle, a farmer in Rushton Spencer, who also owned property in Leek. A document concerning a mortgage transfer in the *Bednall Archive* refers to a house and druggist's shop situated on the South side of Custard Lane in Leek (now Stanley Street) which had been occupied by Hugh Wardle. Letters from a William Wardle at Clitheroe to Hugh Wardle, druggist, Leek, dated 1829, confirm that Hugh Wardle was established in Leek at that time. This William Wardle, a solicitor, is most probably Hugh's brother.
Elizabeth's mother was Elizabeth Young, the daughter of Samuel Young and Thomasina Leeke. To avoid confusion I will refer to Elizabeth Wardle, nee Young, as Elizabeth Wardle, senior, and her daughter as Elizabeth Wardle, junior. Elizabeth, junior, wife of Thomas Wardle, gave the names Young and Leeke as middle names for two of her children.
The Young family were originally curriers in Leek whose business was situated near to The Swan (recently renamed The Green Dragon) in St Edward Street; they owned premises under the Swan Inn and an adjoining house in Spout Street (now St Edward Street), as well as Bank House on Clerk Bank and later Lyme House Farm at Longsdon. By 1861 Elizabeth Wardle, senior, was the owner of the property under the Assembly Room at the Swan Inn. *(Bednall Archive)*
Hugh Wardle, Elizabeth's father, is listed on the 1841 census return as a druggist in the Market Place in Leek, although his wife and children are enumerated at Hallwater Farm in Endon. Hugh Wardle, although still living, is not with his family ten years later when his wife and children are residing in Derby Street in Leek. Elizabeth Wardle 'senior' is working as a governess and her daughter Elizabeth as a teacher. Elizabeth Wardle, senior, is listed in *Whites History, Gazetteer*

Above left
Elizabeth Wardle

Above right
Elizabeth Wardle
with grandson
Lance Worthington

Above
62 St. Edward Street

and *Directory of Staffordshire, 1851*, as the proprietor of an academy in Derby Street where she was prepared to take in boarders. It would appear that the family might have been experiencing financial difficulties. However in 1861 Elizabeth, senior, now a widow, is described as 'a proprietor of houses' when she is visiting her brother Samuel at Lyme House. In June 1867, Mrs Elizabeth Wardle (senior) of Leek had been visiting Lyme House farm and on arising had left on the dressing table a gold watch, a gold eyeglass, a gold seal, a gold ring, a gold key and a glass letter stamp. These valuable items, the property of a woman of substance, were stolen and recovered the same day.

In 1857 Elizabeth Wardle, junior, married Thomas Wardle, a silk dyer, at St Edward's Church in Leek. They made their home in Leekbrook where Joshua Wardle, Thomas's father, had a dye-works. Six children were born at Leekbrook between the years 1858 to 1865, but sadly two of the children died in infancy and a son died when only three years old. Thomas and Elizabeth moved to Leek, in 1866, where eight more children were born, one of these children also died in infancy. After

Right
54 St. Edward Street

the birth of her fourteenth child in 1877, when Elizabeth was almost forty three years old, she suffered a serious illness which made her an invalid for almost two years and resulted in her leaving the family home in Leek and returning to Leekbrook perhaps to be nursed by her husband's relatives. She and her husband, Thomas, founded the Leek Embroidery Society in 1879, shortly after she recovered from this illness, whilst they were living at 62 St Edward Street. Later the large family moved to an elegant Georgian town house further up the street at 54 St Edward Street.

This house is now the solicitor's practice of Bowcock and Pursaill.

By 1879 Elizabeth Wardle was already an accomplished needlewoman who had stitched ecclesiastical embroideries from at least 1864. The alms bags she stitched for St. Edward's church at Cheddleton date from that year. She had supervised a group of women working on church embroideries since 1868. Elizabeth Wardle's name is embroidered at the centre of a tape stitched on to the Pelican frontal, worked for St Luke's church in Leek.

Elizabeth imparted her needlework skills to her pupils in the Leek School of Embroidery and supervised many other needlewomen in projects ranging from church embroideries to the facsimile of the Bayeux Tapestry. She supervised and taught the young needlewomen who worked for the Leek Embroidery Society. An article in the *Leek Times*, dated 1886, reports the opening of a sale of work by Elizabeth Wardle. This article refers to the noble and successful effort she has made, not only to give Leek a name in the world of art, but also to bring art into women's work. She was the superintendent of the Embroidery Society until her death in 1902 and in several Leek Annuals is described as the director of the society.

Elizabeth was a well organized and philanthropic woman who was involved with many charitable societies in Leek. In 1885 she founded the Leek branch of the Sailors and Soldiers Families Association working tirelessly for it during the Boer War. At the time of the birth of her youngest daughter she was the Honorary Secretary of the Leek School of Cookery which was held at 2 Stockwell Street and was the author of '*Easy Dinners Arranged for Young Housekeepers*'. She was also the secretary of the Leek branch of the Church Missionary Society and president of the local branch of the Ministering Children's League.

In 1901 Thomas and Elizabeth Wardle attended a wedding in Leek; among the list of expensive wedding gifts was a Leek embroidered tea- cosy, which was their gift to the bride and groom. An indication of the value placed on Leek Embroidery at that time.

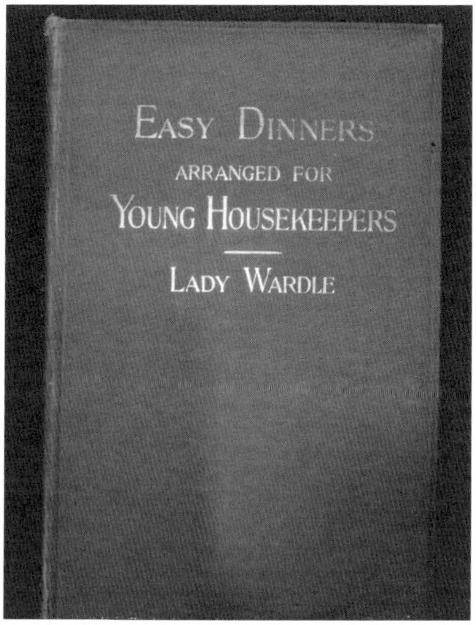

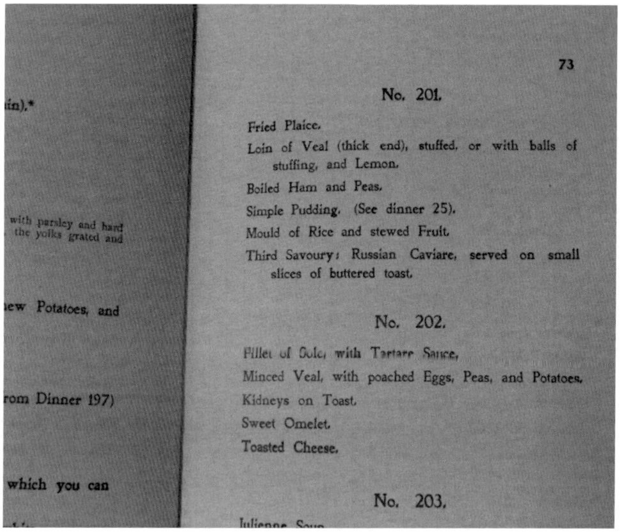

73

No. 201.

Fried Plaice.
Loin of Veal (thick end), stuffed, or with balls of stuffing, and Lemon.
Boiled Ham and Peas.
Simple Pudding. (See dinner 25).
Mould of Rice and stewed Fruit.
Third Savoury: Russian Caviare, served on small slices of buttered toast.

No. 202.

Fillet of Sole, with Tartare Sauce.
Minced Veal, with poached Eggs, Peas, and Potatoes.
Kidneys on Toast.
Sweet Omelet.
Toasted Cheese.

No. 203.

Above
Lady Wardle's book, 'Easy Dinners arranged for Young Housekeepers'

This indomitable woman died in 1902 after a long illness when she was described as having a warm and generous heart and a charming disposition. Many members of the Leek Embroidery Society sent floral tributes to her funeral.

Elizabeth Wardle was involved in all aspects of the Embroidery Society and the School of Embroidery both supervising and stitching exquisite Leek Embroidery.

Martha Phoebe Wardle
1839-1896

Phoebe, as she was always known, was the daughter of Joshua and Mary Wardle and the sister-in-law of Elizabeth Wardle. She never married and lived most of her life at Cheddleton Heath House. Joshua moved here, after 1848, from his house at the side of his dye-works at Leekbrook. When her father died in 1879 he left Phoebe and her sister, Ann, all his household goods, furniture, plate linen, china, musical instruments, beds, bedding and other household effects plus a £1,000 legacy each. The family home and land together with the dye-works and other houses including the "Traveller's Rest" public house were bequeathed to Phoebe's brothers, Thomas and George Wardle. Phoebe and her sister, Ann, continued to live in Cheddleton Heath House after the death of their parents. The house on Cheddleton Heath is a large property with extensive grounds. A turret at one side of the house has a window from which the dye-works could be seen. Joshua Wardle is reputed to have looked out from this window at 10pm, every night, to see a signal from his night watchman indicating that all was well at the works.

The musical Wardle family worshipped at St Edward's church at Cheddleton where, before he moved to Leek, Thomas Wardle had been the first choirmaster, who taught the choir with a concertina. Phoebe became a Sunday school teacher at the church in 1855 and was both choir mistress and organist there for ten years before her death. Phoebe is believed to have stitched the sedilia cushions for the church. When she died *St Edward's Parish Magazine* at Cheddleton described her as a devoted and self-sacrificing member of the church. A beautiful stained glass window was installed in the church at Cheddleton in memory of Phoebe. The central panel of the window fittingly features St Cecilia, the patron saint of music. This panel was paid for by subscriptions from the congregation at the church while Thomas Wardle donated the two side panels in memory of two of his deceased infant children. The Leek Embroidery Society also stitched two

Above
Joshua Wardle
Limited

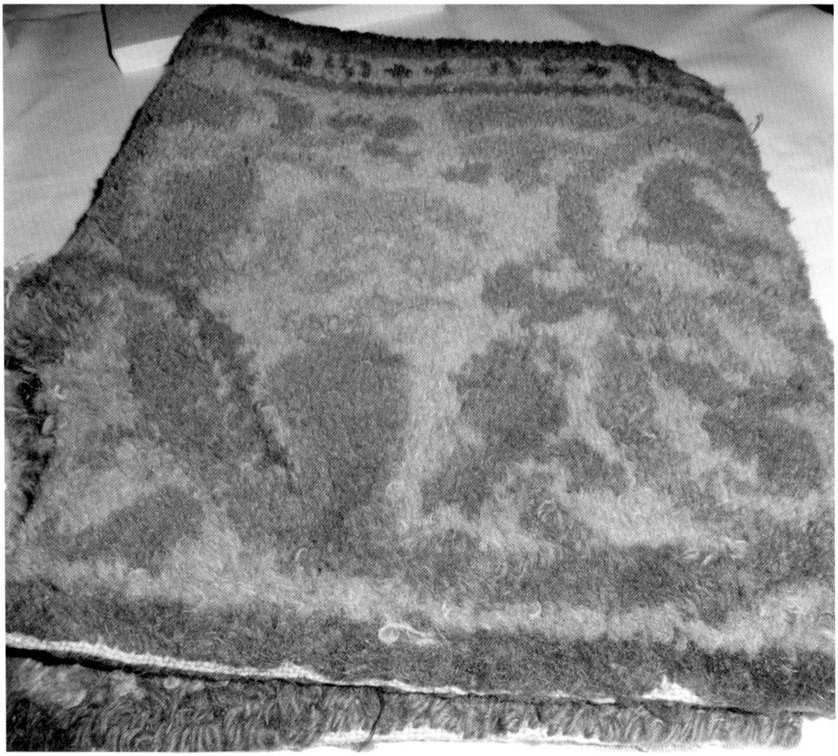

Above, left
Cheddelton Heath House, where Phoebe lived, showing the turret used by Joshua Wardle to survey his factory

Above, **right**
The ornate doorway at Cheddleton Heath House

Right
A remnant of the carpet for St Leonard's church at Ipstones

Above
Cheddleton Church

altar cloths for the church in memory of Phoebe. The white altar cloth, stitched by the Leek Embroidery Society and the East Grinstead Sisterhood, survives and is displayed behind glass in the church at Cheddleton. Unfortunately the green frontal has not survived, however the green fald stool cloth stitched at the same time can still be seen. Phoebe was one of the needlewomen who stitched the 'Four Kings' altar frontal for St Edward's church in Leek. In earlier years Phoebe had worked on a super frontal and altar frontal for St Leonard's church at Ipstones. According to Pam Inder and Marian Aldis in '*Susanna's Carpet*', she represented the Leek Embroiderers when Ipstones church was reopened in 1877. Phoebe is said to have supervised the stitching of a carpet and embroideries for the church as Elizabeth Wardle was incapacitated after the birth of her youngest daughter. Phoebe died at the Wardle family home in 1890.

Lucy Wardle (nee Pidcock)
1871 – 1957

Above
Lucy Wardle at Edith Wardle's wedding

Lucy's parents were Benjamin and Elizabeth Pidcock. Her father had been the vicar of St Luke's church in Leek before he was moved to the Parish of Easton in Hampshire. Lucy married Arthur Henry Wardle, a son of Thomas and Elizabeth Wardle, in Easton, in 1898. Lucy was married in her father's church when she wore a wedding dress of ivory duchess satin with a semi court train. The newly married couple lived in Leek where Arthur became a partner in the family firm known as Sir T & A Wardle which operated from the Churnet Works in Leek. Lucy and Arthur lived at Littlehales on Buxton Road for several years. In 1903, while they were living at Littlehales, Lucy placed an advertisement in the *Leek Times* for an experienced housemaid-waitress. At this time Lucy was a member of the Leek branch of the Primrose League as were several members of the Wardle family. Arthur Wardle died in 1916 when he and Lucy were living at Ford House. After her husband's death Lucy lived at Southfields before moving to Ashcombe Park, a large residence just outside the village of Cheddleton, where she died in 1957.

Both Lucy and her mother stitched the Khartoum frontal in 1905. Her mother, Elizabeth Pidcock, was one of the needlewomen who stitched the Pelican frontal and is included in the Pelican frontal chapter.

Right
Letterhead for the Churnet Dye Works

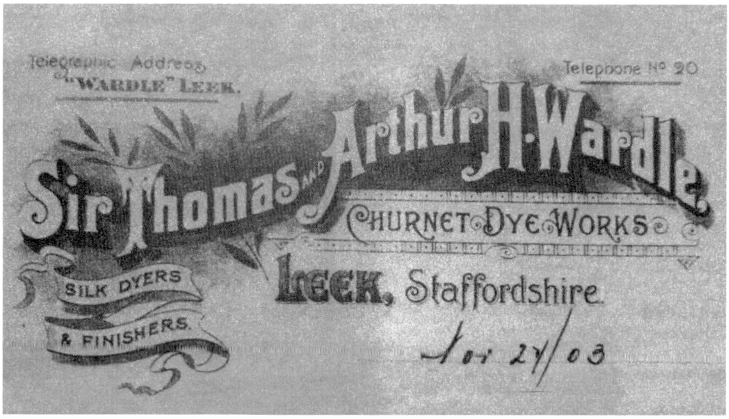

Right
Ford House on the corner of Market Street and Stockwell Street

Ann Wardle (nee Welch)
1869 – 1947

Ann Welch was born in Westhoughton, near Bolton in Lancashire. She was the daughter of Thomas and Elizabeth Welch. Her father was an indigo printer, dyer and finisher who employed over one hundred hands at his Green Vale Printworks in 1881. Ann spent her childhood at Green Vale House, a large property in Westhoughton.

Right
Bridge House at Bridge End in Leek

Right
Hencroft works
(see photo page 16)

When Ann was twenty two years old she married Bernard Wardle, one of the sons of Thomas and Elizabeth Wardle, at St James Church in Westhaughton. Bernard Wardle was a silk and calico printer who was in business at the Hencroft Works in Leek. A letter written by Bernard in 1899 states that he dyed and printed plush, velvets, corahs, silk, cretonnes, chintzes, linens, flax cloth and linings. Ann and Bernard lived at Bridge House at Bridge End in Leek, a substantial property which had fourteen rooms. Ann's father, a wealthy man, died suddenly while he was staying with Ann and Bernard at their home in 1901.

A letter in the *Bednall Archive* dated 1908, written by Leon Solon, invited Ann and Bernard Wardle to dine with him at Abbey Cottage in Leek. The letter indicates that a rubber or two of Bridge might be played.

Ann left Leek when her husband Bernard closed the Hencroft Works and relocated to Pale Meadow, Bridgnorth. Ann and Bernard lived at Danesford in Bridgnorth in a substantial house which had fourteen rooms. Ann Wardle helped to stitch the Khartoum Frontal.

Lydia Young Wardle
1868-1949

Above
Lydia Young Wardle at Edith Wardle's wedding

Lydia was the only one of Thomas and Elizabeth's Wardle's children to remain single. In common with other members of the Wardle family she was a keen amateur thespian. As a member of the Leek Philothespian Club she played a part in their 1891 production of 'She Stoops to Conquer'.
Like her mother before her she worked tirelessly for the community being secretary of 'Waifs and Strays' in 1901 and secretary of the Leek Branch of the Soldiers and Sailors

Right
Red Litany desk fall stitched by Lydia for All Saints Church in Leek

Families Association in 1915. Her mother had founded the Leek branch of this association in 1885. Lydia had many interests including that of horticulture. *The Journal of the Royal Horticultural Society*, in 1895, records Lydia's 3rd class pass in that subject.

Right
Banner at St Peter's Church in Stoke stitched by Lydia Wardle and Clara Bill

Two years after working on the Khartoum frontal she supervised members of the Girls Friendly Society to make a beautiful sanctuary carpet for St Edward's church in Leek. The carpet was stitched to a design by Sir Giles Gilbert Scott and coloured by Lydia's cousin Elcanor Wardle. The wool for the carpet was dyed by Lydia's brother Arthur Henry Wardlc at the Churnet Works dye-works. As an associate of the Girls Friendly Society she made the Bishop's cushion for the church. Lydia was one of a group of women who represented the Leek branch of this society at a meeting in Lichfield in 1912.

Right
Iddesleigh

After her mother, Lady Wardle, died Lydia continued to run the Leek Embroidery Society. Letters now in the local studies archive at Leek Public Library reveal her continuing interest in the Leek Embroidery Society after it ceased to operate in 1930. She corresponded with several people concerning the facsimile of the Bayeux Tapestry, by then located at Reading, which was being exhibited in South Africa in 1935. Lydia was always eager to ensure that the importance of the Leek Embroidery Society and the principal role her mother played in that society was not forgotten.

After the death of her parents Lydia lived at Iddesleigh in Hartington Street, a large house having eight rooms. Later Lydia moved to 8 Spencer Avenue and finally to 2 Southfields where she died in 1949.

Above
2 Southfields

In her will she left a legacy of £100 for a choir arch window. When it was unveiled the choir, the vicar and relatives of Miss Wardle walked in procession to the back of St Luke's Church where Miss Ada Wardle unveiled a plaque to the donor's memory and the vicar dedicated the window.

In the congregation were former members of the Leek School of Embroidery.

Margaret Elizabeth Wardle
1869-1949

Margaret, a daughter of Thomas and Elizabeth Wardle, was born when the family lived at 62 St Edward Street. She was ten years old when the Leek Embroidery Society was founded. Before her marriage she worked with her mother stitching panel 17 of the facsimile of the Bayeux Tapestry before working on the 'Four Kings' altar frontal for St Edward's church. Margaret also stitched a white cope and a set of white chasuble, maniple and stole for All Saints Church which had been designed by her brother Tom Wardle.
Margaret married Philip Jukes Worthington, a Leek silk manufacturer. They first lived in Hugo Street before moving to Stockwell House. Sadly, Philip died in 1902, after being ill for several months. Their son Lance was eleven years old when his father died. Two years later Margaret married Commander Guy Gaunt in Hong Kong. Guy Gaunt had a distinguished career in the navy and was promoted to full Admiral and knighted in 1918. In the early 1920s Sir Guy and Lady Gaunt lived at Gaunts Wood their new name for Swainsley Hall. Swainsley Hall had been her father's country retreat where he had entertained Mark Twain and Lord Baden Powell amongst other celebrities. Margaret and Guy also had a villa in Monte Carlo.
Admiral Guy Gaunt was elected as Member of Parliament for the Buckrose Constituency in the 1922 General Election. In 1923 the *Hull Daily Mail* reported that Lady Gaunt had sustained a serious injury while motoring near her home at Gaunts Wood and had been unable to support her husband at times. Subsequent newspaper reports claimed that she had broken her collar bone in a fall and had an operation on her shoulder. Lady Gaunt went to the Riviera for a few weeks to recuperate.
After her husband was elected Lady Gaunt supported her husband at numerous functions in Bridlington. She accompanied her husband when he gave an address to Bridlington and District Women's Unionist Association.

Right
Margaret Wardle with her first husband Philip Worthington and their son, Lance

Right
Swainsley Hall renamed Gaunts Wood by the Gaunts

Right
Detail from the stole

Far Right
Part of the stole stitched by Lady Gaunt for All Saints Church in Leek

Below
Litany Desk Fall for All Saints Church stitched by Margaret when she was married to Philip Worthington

Afterwards Lady Gaunt spoke to the members and visited the men's club and the bowling green. In 1924 she was present when her husband opened the children's park and recreation ground in Bridlington. On this occasion Sir Guy tried his hand on the putting green while Lady Gaunt played tennis.

Lady Gaunt's marriage ended after 1926 when Guy Gaunt was cited as co-respondent in Sir Richard Cruise's divorce petition. The following year Margaret was granted a decree nisi citing her husband's adultery.

Lady Margaret Gaunt died in an accidental fire in her bedroom at Swainsley Hall in 1949. By this time the property had reverted to its original name. Although Lady Gaunt had sold the property in 1947 she had lived in an eight roomed cottage in the grounds of the hall but at the time of the fire had taken up residence in the hall, which was a hotel at the time. It is believed that a coal fire near to her bed started the blaze which destroyed the west wing of the hotel.

Margaret E Wardle is included in a list of names of women who stitched the Four Kings Frontal. This cannot be verified and as Margaret married Phillip Worthington in 1889 it casts doubt on the authenticity of this list.

Edith Wardle
1872-1925

Edith, one of the daughters of Thomas and Elizabeth, was born while the family lived at 62 St Edward Street in Leek. She would have been just six years old when William Morris last stayed with the family at that house. Morris was working on natural dyes with her father at the Hencroft dye-works. In common with her siblings Edith was a keen amateur thespian, taking part in a 'Grand Dramatic Concert' at the Town Hall in Leek in aid of charity and, in 1891, was a member of the cast of 'She Stoops to Conquer' staged by the Leek Philothespian Club.

Edith married Walter Robert Underhill at St Edward's church in Leek in 1902 just a few weeks before her mother died. Her husband was an electrical engineer who grew up in Oxford. He was trained by Sir Charles Bright and took part in two cable laying expeditions on the west coast of Africa in the mid 1880s. Walter Underhill's sister, Ida, was a teacher of art embroidery and church work [sic]. Edith's wedding was described as a quiet occasion owing to serious illness in the family. This may have referred to her mother or to her brother-in-law, Philip Worthington, who died in September after a long illness. However Edith was attended by five bridesmaids and a page and her wedding ceremony included a full choral service. Her father had composed 'Music for the form of Solemnization of Holy Matrimony' for the earlier wedding of her sister, Margaret, and this music was also used at Edith's wedding.
Edith wore a dress of ivory brocade manufactured by Messrs. Warner & sons of Spitalfields and Braintree. The dress was trimmed with duchess lace, a wedding gift from Mr. and Mrs. Edward Challinor. Edward was the local solicitor who later organized the production of an altar frontal for the Gordon Memorial church in Khartoum.

Above
Edith Wardle's wedding day. This photograph was taken in the garden of 54 St Edward Street in Leek. Elizabeth Wardle is seated second from the left on the front row. Thomas Wardle is on the extreme left of the second row

After their marriage Edith and Walter moved to Lenzie in Scotland where Walter worked as an electrical engineer and contractor and where their children were born. Their daughter, Joan, married the Scottish architect, Mervyn Noad and their son Michael Leeke Underhill relocated to New Zealand where he became the Dean of Christchurch Cathedral.

Elizabeth Leeke Wardle
1877-1946

Above
Mrs Horace Wardle formerly Elizabeth Leeke Wardle

Elizabeth was the youngest child of Thomas and Elizabeth Wardle. She was a baby when William Morris stayed in their home when experimenting with natural dyes with her father and just two years old when the Leek Embroidery Society began. She lived at the family home in St Edward Street before marrying her cousin Horace Townley Wardle, in 1901. Horace was the son of her father's brother, George Wardle, from Leekbrook.
Her wedding reception was held in the family home at 54 St Edward Street. In the early years of their marriage Horace and Elizabeth lived at 12 Hugo Street which, when it was offered for sale in 1902, was described as a large and convenient villa residence, built in the Elizabethan style. The couple later moved to Ladydale, a spacious residence with extensive grounds, where occasionally Elizabeth supervised sporting contests in the grounds for both guides and scouts. She was very involved in the Girl Guide Movement acting as the county commissioner. In 1920, Robert Baden Powell dined with Horace and Elizabeth at Ladydale before going to Beggars Lane cricket ground where scouts and guides from all over the district had gathered. Elizabeth was actively engaged in many Leek organizations being the honorary secretary of the Leek branch of the Ministering Childrens League and the Leek Primrose League. In the 1920s, Elizabeth collected the names of Leek's fallen soldiers from the Great War, which were to be displayed on the new Nicholson War Memorial. Lists were on display for several weeks together with advertisements in the local press to ensure that every name was collected.

During the second World War she was the president and secretary of Leek Soldiers and Sailors Family Association and had a similar post on the War Pensions Committee. Elizabeth was also a Commissioner of the Peace.

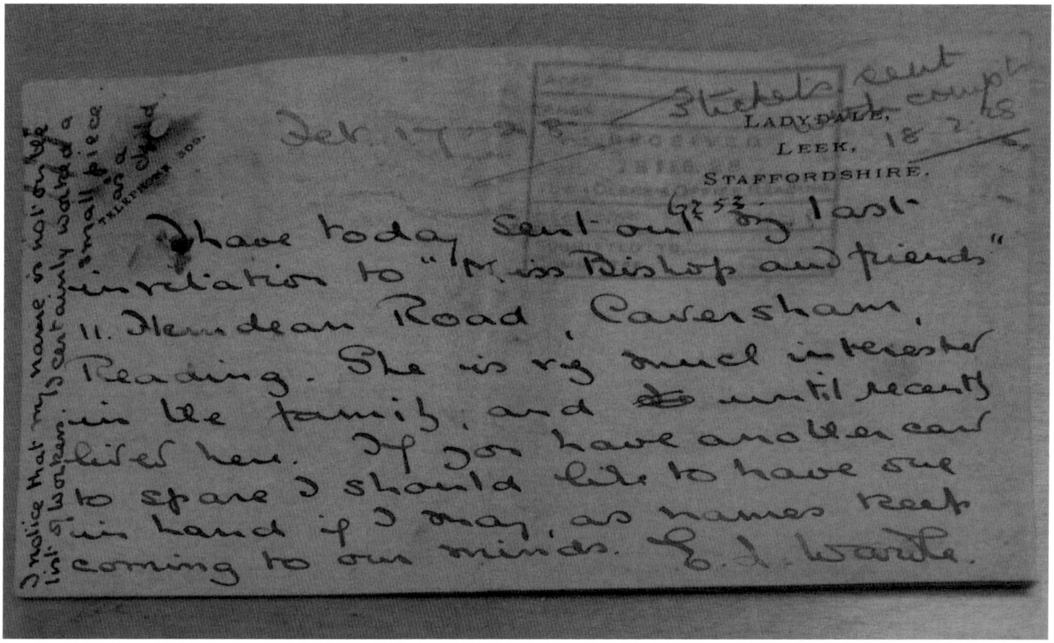
LADYDALE,
LEEK,
STAFFORDSHIRE.
TELEPHONE 200.

Feb. 17 '28

3 tickets sent compl. 18.2.28

I have today sent out my last invitation to "Miss Bishop and friends" 11. Henleydean Road, Caversham, Reading. She is very much interested in the family, and until recently lived here. If you have another card to spare I should like to have one in hand if I may, as names keep coming to our minds. E. L. Wardle.

I notice that my name is not on the list of workers. I certainly worked a small piece on a shield

Above
Letter from Elizabeth Leeke Wardle

Throughout her life she was a steadfast churchwoman actively involved at St Edward's church and later closely identified with work in All Saints Parish where she and her husband resided. Elizabeth Leeke Wardle's name is not attached to any known Leek Embroidery but is included here as it would be most unusual for her to be the only one of Elizabeth Wardle's daughters who did not stitch. A note, written by Elizabeth, on an invitation to attend Reading Museum in 1928 reveals that she did work on a small piece of the facsimile of the Bayeux Tapestry.

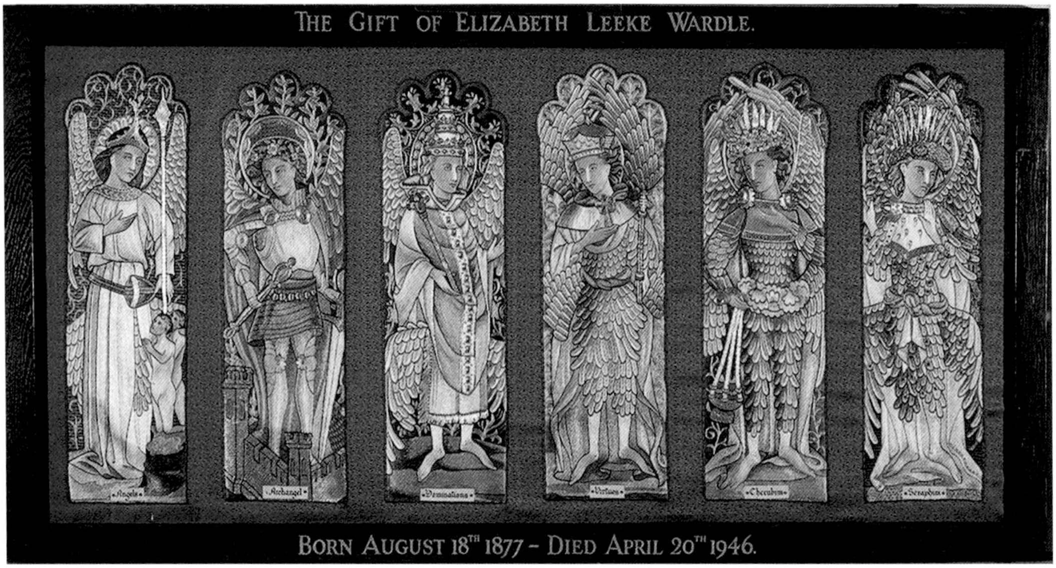

THE GIFT OF ELIZABETH LEEKE WARDLE.
BORN AUGUST 18TH 1877 - DIED APRIL 20TH 1946.

Above
A panel of angels in St Edward's church in Leek presented by Elizabeth Leeke Wardle

The Leekbrook Wardles

Frances Martha Wardle (nee Bray)
1841–1923
Eleanor Wardle
1865-1947
Mildred Wardle
1867-1958
Grace Wardle
1871-1954
Ada Mary Wardle
1873-1956

Ada, Eleanor, Grace and Mildred Wardle were sisters, daughters of George and Francis Wardle. George Wardle was Thomas Wardle's brother who was in partnership with him and continued to operate the dye-works at Leekbrook under the name of Joshua Wardle & Sons. His wife Frances was born in Chiswick, although they married at Cheddleton in 1864. Frances's father and grandfather were builders, who had several employees, in London. Her father's name was 'Horatio' which perhaps explains why her only son was named Horace. She worshipped at St Edward's church at Cheddleton and was a generous contributor to the church helping to defray the costs of altar frontals and hangings. Frances was also a needlewoman and stitched alms bags for St Luke's church in Leek. After George died Frances continued to live at Leekbrook with her daughters. She died there in 1923 the same year her great nephew Lance Worthington married. Many members of the Wardle family attended the wedding and the presents received by the bride and groom were listed in the local newspaper. Frances, now aged 82, presented the happy couple with a pair of old swords! Frances is buried in the churchyard of St Edward's church at Cheddleton with her husband and daughters.

George and Frances Wardle had four daughters and one son; their son, Horace, married his cousin Elizabeth Leeke Wardle, the youngest daughter of Thomas and Elizabeth Wardle.

Grace Wardle was the only one of the four girls to marry; she wed her cousin Charles Illsley when she was in her forties. The sisters spent most of their lives in the family home at Leekbrook House, situated between Leek and Cheddleton. As young women they attended art classes in Leek and were keen amateur thespians. Eleanor (Nellie) Wardle was on the executive council of Leek's branch of the Primrose League (Cruso Habitation) eventually becoming the ruling councillor. Both Eleanor and her sister, Ada, who became the Dame President, were elected to represent Staffordshire on the Primrose League Grand Council for several years. Eleanor worked the hangings for the pulpit and Litany Stool for Cheddleton church in 1892. They were made to match the purple altar frontal made for the church by Elizabeth Wardle. Grace was the honorary secretary of the Leek branch of 'Missions to Seamen' and with the help of her cousin Lydia Wardle, arranged a Grand Ballad Concert at the Town Hall in Leek in aid of charity. The sisters stitched Leek Embroidery for themselves and to give as presents. The report of the wedding of Jessica Challinor to Albert Muntz in 1898 lists wedding presents given to the bride and groom. Nellie Wardle gave a photograph holder in Leek Embroidery and Mildred a Leek Embroidery cushion. Nellie and Ada Wardle were both associates of the Girls Friendly Society who made the Sanctuary carpet for St Edward's church in Leek. The design for the carpet was coloured by Eleanor and Ada worked with others on the communicants' kneeler.
The sisters attended many social functions in Leek including a fancy dress ball held in 1905 in aid of Leek's Cottage Hospital and a garden party at Westwood Hall in 1910.

Right
Leekbrook House now divided into apartments

The house at Leekbrook where the sisters lived with their parents was a large valuable property. George Wardle insured it with the Imperial Insurance Company Limited in 1892. The contents of the house were also insured, one of the named individual items insured was an oil painting by Rembrandt valued then at £50.
Leekbrook House was advertised for sale in 1928 when it comprised three reception rooms and eight bedrooms. Now divided into four apartments, remains of its former past are indicated by traces of elaborate plaster ceilings and cornices, large rooms and the former imposing entrance.
The sisters moved to a house at 1, Southfields in Leek in later life and began to worship at All Saints church. In 1910 they decorated the chancel for the wedding of Miss M Partridge. Miss Partridge was the sister of the curate at All Saints and Ada Wardle was one of her bridesmaids.
Eleanor, Mildred, Grace and Ada Wardle all helped to stitch the Khartoum Frontal.

More Extraordinary Embroiderers

Needlewomen have been included in previous chapters according to their known work on specific projects. Several women are included here as they stitched individual pieces, or are known to have stitched fire screens and other items for their homes or have established embroidery businesses in the town. Descendants of several of these women claim that their relatives were members of the Leek Embroidery Society. As previously stated this is difficult to confirm as no records survive detailing membership of the Society.

Background Image
Detail from Altar frontals at St Chad's Church in Longsdon

ihr

The Brealey Firescreen

During the 'Extraordinary Leek Embroidery Society' exhibition, in the summer of 2013, a descendant of the Brealey family, whose ancestors once lived in Leek, brought in a fire screen thought to have been stitched by an ancestor. This beautiful fire screen features Leek Embroidery. It is not known whether the woman who stitched it was a member of the Leek Embroidery Society or whether she purchased a pattern from the Society which she stitched at home. Neither is it possible to definitely identify which of the Brealey women stitched it. However, a photograph of the fire screen inside Burns Croft, a house in Leek, presents an interesting clue.
Reginald Woodhouse Brealey and his wife Ellen, nee Walley, lived at Burnscroft after their marriage. Ellen lived there until her death in 1951. Was Ellen the needlewoman who stitched this exquisite fire screen? She was born in Hanley in 1876 to William Walley, a corn merchant, and his wife, Ellen. Her mother was a Lockett whose family had farmed at Red Earth farm, near Leek, for many years. Could the family have kept up their connections with Leek and been in contact with the Leek Embroidery Society?
Equally, and perhaps more likely, it might have been stitched by Reginald Woodhouse Brearley's mother. She was Frances Sarah Brealey, the wife of Thomas Brealey, a land agent and surveyor in Leek, who designed both Leek's Butter Market and Fire Station. Frances was born in 1855 and married in 1877, moving to Leek from Cheadle and living in the town when the Embroidery Society was founded. As the wife of a well known businessman in Leek she would have known many of the wives and daughters of silk manufacturers and solicitors who were members of the Society.

Above
Brealey fire screen
in Burnscroft

Susan Carding (later Cumming)
born 1877

Myra Carding
1873 – 1954

Susan was one of ten children born to Micah and Hannah Carding and is listed as an art embroiderer on both the 1891and 1901 census returns. Descendants of Susan are aware that she stitched Leek Embroidery and was a member of the Embroidery Society. It is possible that she worked for the society at the shop in St Edward Street. A cushion cover embroidered by her is now in the hands of a private collector. Susan's sister, Myra, may also have stitched Leek Embroidery. Many Leek residents will remember the Misses Keates who had a wool shop in Stanley Street and who were descended from one of Susan's sisters.

The girls' father, Micah, was a master plumber and painter who had a shop at 3 Market Place in Leek, where the family also lived. The shop no longer survives having been replaced by modern buildings. Micah was a successful tradesman who employed four men and four apprentices in his business in 1881. He was connected with Leek's Fire Brigade for many years holding positions as both Captain and Chief Officer. Susan's brothers Joseph and Albert were both long serving members of Leek Fire Brigade too.

In 1904 Susan married William Cumming at St Edward's Church in Leek. William worked in a braid warehouse but his father, James, had worked as a block printer. William and his siblings were born in Ireland and lived there before moving to Leek. In 1891, the family lived in Abbey Green Road near to the Hencroft Print Works and the Churnet Works. Perhaps James Cumming was one of Thomas Wardle's block printers. Although William stayed in Leek his parents moved to Dartford, where James pursued his career as a block printer. After her marriage Susan, now Mrs. Cumming, went into business operating an Art Needlework Depot in the Market Place. In several *Kelly's Post Office Directories* and in the

Above
The Carding sisters, Susan Carding stands on the back row with her sister, Myra, on her right

Above
The Carding Shop at the top of Leek's Market Place. Until recently the site was occupied by Leek Tourist Information Centre

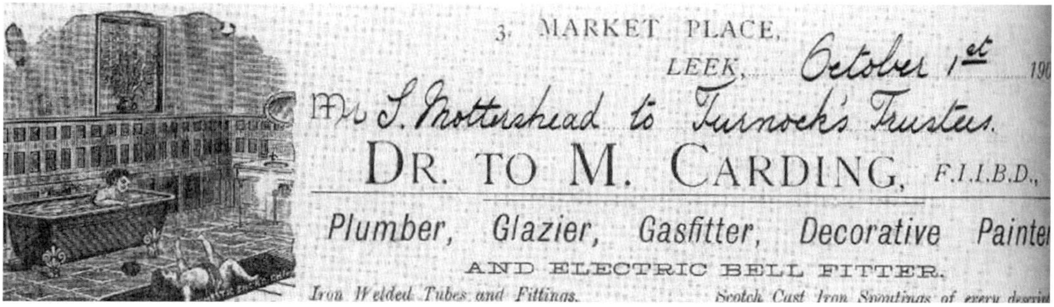

3, MARKET PLACE,
LEEK, October 1st 190
Mr S. Mottershead to Turnock's Trustees.
DR. TO M. CARDING, F.I.I.B.D.,
Plumber, Glazier, Gasfitter, Decorative Painte
AND ELECTRIC BELL FITTER.
Iron Welded Tubes and Fittings. Scotch Cast Iron Spoutings of every descri

Above
Carding bill-head

Leek Annuals she is also listed as an art needle worker in Stockwell Street. She placed an advertisement in the *Leek Times* in August 1907 informing potential customers that her Leek Art Depot at 13 Stockwell Street was now open for business. She gives her occupation on the 1911 census return as 'art needle worker' and reveals that she is an employer who works from her home.

Myra Carding is also thought to have stitched Leek Embroidery. In 1902 she was awarded first prize for needlework at the School of Art in the Nicholson Institute. She was a pupil teacher as a young woman but for most of her life did not work. She lived with her parents in the Market Place before moving with her father, after he retired, to 14 Westwood Road where she died.

Anne Cruso
1812 – 1893

Anne Cruso (nee Searight) was born in Liverpool, the daughter of a wealthy Irish merchant. The Searight family had connections with Leek as Anne's mother was Betty Ford, the daughter of Hugh Ford, who lived at Ford House. Anne married John Cruso, in 1851, when she was almost forty years old and in receipt of a private income. John Cruso, who was more than twenty years her senior, lived at Foxlowe, the elegant Georgian house at the top of Leek's Market Place. He was a wealthy,

Right
Foxlowe

respected solicitor who was a magistrate, an Improvement Commissioner and a deputy Lieutenant for Staffordshire. After John Cruso died, in 1867, Anne stayed on at Foxlowe efficiently running the large house and extensive grounds with the help of a cook, housekeeper, housemaids, kitchen maids, laundry maid and a coachman. She treated her servants well and they remained in her employment for many years. Anne Cruso played a prominent role in the life of the town opening bazaars and entertaining important visitors, including the Earl and Countess of Macclesfield, bishops and members of parliament. She was the patron of a number of organizations and laid several foundation stones, including that of All Saints church. When the library opened in 1884 she was issued the first book as a mark of respect. In 1886, Reverend Pownoll

Right
Ann Cruso

Phipps travelled to Leek to marry his son to Jessica Mabel Challinor (another Leek needlewoman). He and his wife stayed with Anne Cruso, he later recorded in his diary that she was a very nice and rich old lady.

Foxlowe still stands at the head of Leek's Market Place and is now an Arts Centre, the former grounds form part of Leek's Brough Park.

A letter written by Elizabeth Wardle, in 1881, reveals that Anne helped to embroider a handkerchief bag in tussur silk, which was presented to the Princess of Wales. She also presented a pearl, cut in half, which was taken by Surgeon General Cruso off the arm of Tippo Sahib, when he was killed at the taking of Seringapatam. Surgeon General Thomas Cruso was her husband's uncle.

Ellen Dilworth (nee Bennison)
born 1862

Ellen was the daughter of Robert Bennison and Catherine Young and was related to the Wardle family as her mother was Elizabeth Wardle's cousin. The Bennison's lived at Mill Meece, a village near Eccleshall in Staffordshire. In 1881 Robert Bennison farmed 221 acres there. Ellen married Frederick Dilworth at St James Church at Cotes Heath in 1885. Tragically her husband died four years after their marriage leaving Ellen with two young children. Ellen and her children moved to Leek to live with her aunt, Sarah Young, at her house in Hugo Street. Sarah Young was also Elizabeth Wardle's cousin. Ellen stayed on in the house in Hugo Street after her Aunt Sarah left Leek. While living there she helped to stitch the purple altar frontal and super frontal for All Saints Church designed by Tom, the son of Thomas and Elizabeth Wardle. She also stitched a green lectern fall for All Saints church. Her aunt, Sarah Young, was one of the needlewomen who stitched the Four Kings altar frontal which can be seen in the parlour of St Edward's church in Leek.

Right
Detail from the purple altar frontal in All Saints church. Designed by Tom Wardle and stitched by Ellen Dilworth

Mary Ellen (Nellie) McDonough
1877-1953

Above
Nellie McDonough

Nellie was born in Leek in 1877, the daughter of Thomas and Jane McDonough. The family who were of Irish descent had settled in Leek after the disastrous potato famine in Ireland. The McDonough family lived in Leeds for a few years in the early 1880s but had settled back in Leek by 1883 and eventually made their home at 6 North Street. Thomas was a domestic gardener when living in both Leeds and Leek but by the time of the 1911 census he was both groom and gardener. Members of the McDonough family lived in North Street until at least 1964. Nellie was only eleven years old when she is pictured with Elizabeth Wardle and other girls in 1888. She described herself as a hand embroiderer on census returns and very helpfully states that her occupation is 'Leek Embroidery Society' in 1891.

The McDonough's were a Catholic family and Nellie stitched at least two items for St Mary's Catholic Church in Leek. She is reputed to have stitched a picture frame to one of Elizabeth Wardle's designs. The author's grandmother lived next door to the family in North Street and often spoke of Nellie McDonough who worked for the Embroidery Society.

Most of Nellie's siblings were employed in Leek's flourishing silk industry as silk markers, silk folders, silk labellers and silk pattern card wrappers. Annie, one of Nellie's sisters was a prominent member of the Leek Women Workers Union who became vice president in 1907. Later that year she became president of the union, a position she held until 1912 making her the longest serving president. No doubt Nellie would have accompanied her sister to tea dances she organized in the Town Hall on behalf of the Women Workers Union.

Nellie was one of seven children; none of the five girls married and at least three of them died as elderly spinsters at 6, North Street. A family member remembers the old ladies who were very fond of dining on mashed potatoes in the evenings!

Right
North Street houses

Right
The McDonough family, Nellie is seated on the left

Geraldine Maud
1848-1927

Geraldine Maude was the daughter of Alexander and Ellen Donovan; she spent her childhood at Framfield Place an 'elegant mansion in Sussex' situated on the brow of a wooded hill and enjoying extensive views. Her father was a wealthy landowner, a magistrate and a deputy lieutenant of Sussex. As a child Geraldine was looked after by nurses and educated by a governess. The family employed a plethora of servants including a butler, footman, cook, lady's maid, housemaids, kitchen maids and a coachman. Geraldine gave up this privileged life when she married Charles Bulmer Maude who worked in South Africa where he was the rector of Kimberley. Geraldine endured hard times in Kimberley living and working in primitive conditions. According to Lewis and Edwards, Charles Maude wrote "We have a canvas house for our sitting room and a wooden one for our bedroom. The floors are made of brick dried in the sun, but the legs of beds or tables make holes in them." The church had an iron roof and a mud floor, Geraldine commented that when it rained the noise was so loud that they had to give up the services as they could not be heard. They also held day and Sunday school in the church as they didn't have a schoolhouse. Despite this, in true missionary spirit, she thought that they weren't too badly off as they had a choir and a full choral service and the church was crowded every Sunday. A blow struck when a new church, which they had been looking forward to moving into, blew down in a whirlwind. This new church had been imported from England. Geraldine wrote "that those who saw it say it was lifted three feet from the ground and dropped, utterly shapeless, like a street of card houses! And all our money gone, diamonds are down, and times are bad!" However the situation improved and according to William Crisp, in 1880, Bishop Webb of Bloemfontein dedicated the "re-erected 'church-like' church". C. B. Maude served as the third incumbent of St Cyprian's Church in Kimberley from 1877 to 1881.

Ill health forced the Maude's to return to England where Charles was appointed as the Perpetual Curate of Wilnecote

Right
Reverend Maude

before being ordained as the vicar at St Edward's Church in Leek. They lived in the vicarage at Leek, from 1887 to 1896, with domestic staff including a footman, cook and housemaid. While Geraldine and Charles were in Leek her husband established an institute, which comprised a working men's club and a young men's union, in the former St Edward's School on Clerk Bank. In 1896, Charles Maude conveyed the building to trustees; we know it today as the Maude Institute.

Geraldine Maude would have been greatly involved in the local community, supporting her husband and working for the benefit of his parishioners. In addition to his parochial activities CB Maude was the first recorded President of Leek Golf club. In 1891 the Maude's travelled from Leek to Hove where Charles Maude assisted the Bishop of Shrewsbury at the marriage of Ethel Donovan, Geraldine's youngest sister. Ethel married Frederick Stamer, who was a clergyman at Kingsley, a village in the Staffordshire Moorlands.

After leaving Leek Charles was ordained as the vicar of St Chad's in Shrewsbury and later became Archdeacon of Salop. In 1900 he was appointed Prebendary of Gaia Minor in Lichfield Cathedral. In 1911 Geraldine accompanied her husband to the opening of the new Shropshire County Sanatorium, opened by Princess Alexander of Teck. This would have been just one of many official engagements they attended together.

Charles Bulmer Maude died in 1927 at The Castle in Ludlow. Geraldine died there just two years later.

While living in Leek Geraldine helped to stitch the white frontal now displayed in the parlour at St Edward's church in Leek.

Margaret Ann Rigby
1862 – 1933

As a child Margaret lived with her parents at 8 Derby Street in Leek where her father, Joseph Rigby, worked as a master shoemaker. He manufactured shoes at his premises in Derby Street employing nine shoemakers. After Joseph died his widow continued to run the business until the family moved to Athlone Villa at 6 Hugo Street. The villa is a prestigious semi detached property designed by William Sugden, Leek's arts and crafts architect. Although Ann Rigby, Margaret's mother, had her own income after her husband had died, Margaret and her brothers had to work. By 1891, Margaret is working for herself running an embroidery business from Hugo Street. After her mother's death Margaret moved to 76 Southbank Street where she had her own art embroidery business employing a girl to help her. An advertisement in 1918 reveals that she specialized in church embroidery. Margaret's fancy repository in Southbank Street operated until at least 1929.

The Rigby family is of interest as they had connections with both silk and design, Margaret's eldest brother, Joseph Thomas, worked as a chemist in a local print works as a young man before working as a company secretary in a Leek silk mill.

Another brother, George Robert Rigby, first worked as a shoemaker for his father. He attended Art Classes at the Mechanics Institute in Russell Street in Leek and was judged 'satisfactory in drawing and painting'. In 1881, when the Leek Art Classes prizes were presented at the Temperance Hall, it was announced that George had succeeded in obtaining an art teachers certificate. The William Morris Labour Church which opened in Leek, in 1896, had a richly embroidered silk book-cloth which was stitched by an unidentified member of the Leek Embroidery Society and partly designed by George R Rigby. George taught art and worked as an art designer, he opened a studio in Uttoxeter working as a wallpaper designer. In 1911 he described himself as a designer for the artistic trades and an art master.

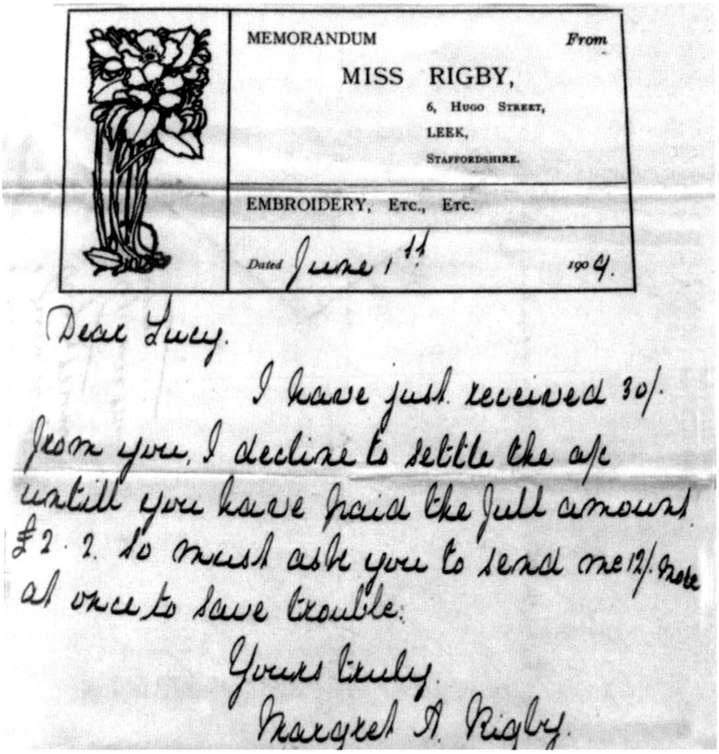

MEMORANDUM From

MISS RIGBY,

6, Hugo Street,

Leek,

Staffordshire.

EMBROIDERY, Etc., Etc.

Dated June 1st 1904.

Dear Lucy.

I have just received 30/. from you, I decline to settle the a/c untill you have paid the full amount £2. 2. so must ask you to send me 12/. note at once to save trouble.

Yours truly.

Margaret A. Rigby.

Right
Invoice from
Margaret Rigby

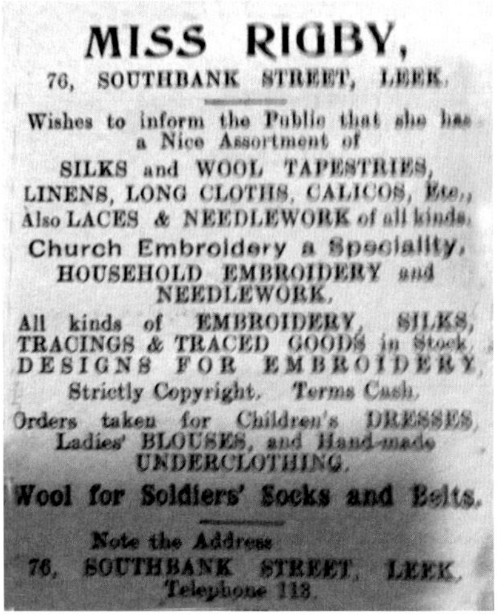

MISS RIGBY,

76, SOUTHBANK STREET, LEEK.

Wishes to inform the Public that she has a Nice Assortment of SILKS and WOOL TAPESTRIES, LINENS, LONG CLOTHS, CALICOS, Etc., Also LACES & NEEDLEWORK of all kinds.

Church Embroidery a Speciality.

HOUSEHOLD EMBROIDERY and NEEDLEWORK.

All kinds of EMBROIDERY, SILKS, TRACINGS & TRACED GOODS in Stock.

DESIGNS FOR EMBROIDERY Strictly Copyright. Terms Cash.

Orders taken for Children's DRESSES, Ladies' BLOUSES, and Hand-made UNDERCLOTHING.

Wool for Soldiers' Socks and Belts.

Note the Address

76, SOUTHBANK STREET, LEEK.

Telephone 113.

Right
Advert from the
Leek Times

Above
The former Rigby home and shoe manufactory in Derby Street

Margaret's younger brother John Scarratt Rigby worked as a silk warehouseman before becoming a designer. He designed the Four Kings altar frontal for St Edward's church in Leek under the direction of his father- in-law George Young Wardle. By 1889 John had left Leek moving to London where he married Mary Wardle, known as Kitten, the daughter of George Young Wardle and niece of Elizabeth Wardle. George was the manager of William Morris's company and was Elizabeth Wardle's brother. The Rigby's lived in Bloomsbury where John worked as a designer for manufacturers and decorators. He is believed to have been estranged from his wife and is living alone in Fulham in 1901 working for himself as a decorative artist. Although he died in England he had lived for some time in Cape Town.

Annie Maria Rowley
1872 – 1921

Above
Annie Maria Rowley

Annie Rowley was the daughter of Thomas Rowley and his wife Zilpha, nee Noble. Zilpha died in 1876 leaving Thomas, who was a silk dyer, to raise four young children. Thomas remarried a year after his wife's death but the family did not stay together. Annie's elder brother, Arthur, did live with his father and his new wife as did her younger sister, Mary Ellen, but Annie and her brother, James, did not. The death of his wife would have been a difficult time for Thomas so he sent his eldest son, James, who was seven years old, to live with his Noble grandparents. Annie, who was only four, seems to have been boarded out as she lived with different families in both 1881, when she was just eight years old, and in 1891. Neither of the families appears to be related to her. However the family was not estranged as Thomas is living with his eldest son, James, in Oldham in 1911.

Annie Maria Rowley was one of Elizabeth Wardle's needlewomen and in 1891 is working as an embroideress [sic]. She married William Chatwin in 1894 and by 1898 had moved with him and their two daughters to Handsworth. In 1911 Annie's husband was a schools attendance officer in Handsworth.

The Stretch Firescreen

This finely stitched fire screen may be the work of Elizabeth Stretch who was born in Leek in 1866. By 1891 she was working as an embroiderer. Both her husband and her father worked in the silk industry and were skilled silk ballers.

Below
Stretch Fire Screen detail

Ann Walker
1868-1959

Ann was born at 19 Canal Street in Leek (now Broad Street) one of the eleven children of William and Elizabeth Walker. Her father was a successful brewer and wine merchant. Before Ann was twelve years old the Walker family had moved to 26 Alsop Street.

In 1908 she married Thomas Grace the son of Thomas Grace, senior, who founded T Grace & Son and who built many of Leek's buildings including the Police Station in Leonard Street, the Fire Station in Stockwell Street and the Butter Market. Ann's husband however did not join his father's building company and worked as a printer and stationer. Ann was forty when she married Thomas who was fifty one, they didn't have children.

Ann Grace was known to her nieces as a rather formidable women who they always referred to as 'The Aunt'. Her niece, Joan Cooper, now in her nineties can remember going with her aunt in the 1920s to the shop at 21 St Edward Street to choose embroidery patterns and threads. This was the shop run by Clara Bill who ran it on behalf of the Embroidery Society. Joan remembers Clara Bill as being a rather plump lady who wore her hair fastened up into a bun. Joan would sit on a chair in the shop while 'The Aunt' discussed colours with Clara Bill before making her purchases. Ann Grace, nee Walker, embroidered throughout her life and was working on a piece of embroidery when she died at the age of ninety. It was well known within the family that Ann Grace had been a member of the Leek Embroidery Society; they are certain that she would not have been paid for her work or stitched work for sale. According to her relatives "the Grace family were well off and selling embroidered pieces would have been frowned on."

Ann was related to another of the Leek needlewomen who was a member of the Embroidery Society as her husband's sister, Ellen, had married John Joseph Bentley. John Joseph's sister was Emma Jane Bentley. Leek families are often distantly

Right
Walker fire screen

Right
A full load ready to be delivered

related and it is not surprising that family members would have similar interests and perhaps encourage each other to become members of the Embroidery Society.

Ann Grace died at 9 Dampier Street in 1959.

Beatrice Ethel Warren (nee Charles)

1866-1955

Beatrice Ethel Charles was the daughter of John Smith Charles and his wife, Ann. The Charles family were principal land owners in Pelsall, living at Pelsall Hall until 1917. The hall was sold to Walsall Health Authority for use as a consumptive sanatorium, today it is a care home. Beatrice Charles grew up at the hall where her father, a landed proprietor, employed several servants including a governess, cook, housemaid and a groom. John Smith Charles' income came from rented property and land, including the land leased by the Pelsall Hall Colliery. Beatrice's brothers were both educated at Rugby School. Her brother, John, became the consulting physician at Bristol Royal Infirmary while Michael was a land agent at Pelsall.

Below
Details from altar frontals at St Chad's church in Longsdon, near Leek, stitched by Mrs. Warren

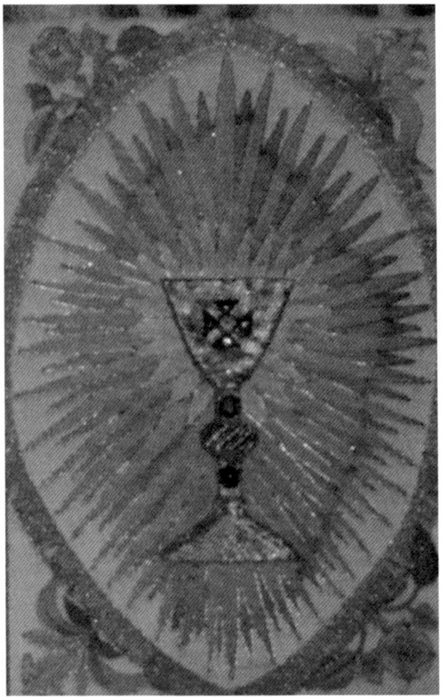

Above
Beatrice Warren

Beatrice appears to have been a devout young woman, writing in 1894 'Songs in the Night' dedicated 'to the sorrowful' in memory of the Reverend Richard McGregor Grier, whom she describes as her spiritual father, teacher, guide and friend. The booklet comprised 15 sonnets to his memory. When Annie Charles, Beatrice's older sister married, in 1896, Richard Grier's widow and daughter were among the guests. Annie had married William Climpson who was the vicar at St Michael's church in Pelsall. The church has stained glass windows in memory of both John Smith Charles and William Climpson. In later life Beatrice's younger sister, Laura Theresa, became a nun in the Society of the Sisters of Bethany, an Anglican religious order.

Beatrice Charles also married a clergyman, Reverend Stephen Percy Warren, who was a curate at Cannock when they married in 1896. Their eldest children were born at Hopwas, near Tamworth, where Stephen Warren was the priest in charge. In 1900 the Warren family moved to Longsdon, a village near Leek, where Stephen was again the priest in charge. However, when St Chad's church was built in 1905

Above
Details from Alter Frontal at St Chad's Church in Longsdon

he became the first vicar at Longsdon, a position he held until 1923. While in Longsdon Beatrice founded a branch of the Mothers Union and became a general and diocesan speaker for the Mothers Union.

St Chad's church was designed by Gerald Horsley who also designed the textiles for the interior of the church. Beatrice Warren stitched green, violet and white altar frontals for the church to Horsley's designs, which are still used today. Among other pieces she stitched, designed by Horsley, was an altar frontal for Zanzibar Cathedral when her son, Hugh, was a priest in the 1920s.

Beatrice Warren took up the pen again in the 1920s writing 'My Beloved', Meditations on the Mystical Types of Our Lord in 1922 and 'St. Peter and the Keys', a study by an Anglo-Catholic in 1928.

When the Warren family left Longsdon they moved into Leek where they lived at 3 Southfields part of an imposing Victorian Terrace. Mrs Warren's obituary in the *Leek Post* in 1955 refers to the work of this prolific needlewoman, who continued to stitch exquisite embroidery until shortly before her death. In addition to the frontals described above the obituary lists other work including a frontal for All Saints church in Hanley, a dorsal for Yarlet Hall school chapel, a

Right
The Warren's with their son, Hugh

banner and chasuble for Holy Trinity in Hadley, Shropshire and an embroidered angel which is now on display at All Saints church in Leek. The obituary also refers to a banner depicting St Michael and a dragon.

Geoff Browne, then a fledgling reporter for the local newspaper, recalls visiting the house in Southfields and speaking to the Warren daughters, Stephanie and Hermione, in order to compile their mother's obituary. He was somewhat taken aback to be taken to see Mrs Warren's body laid out in a bedroom with candles burning around her. He remembers that the Misses Warren went to some lengths to show their family's social status, including an explanation of why their mother's father was entitled to be called 'esquire.' They went into much more detail than could be accommodated in an ordinary newspaper report.

Stephanie and Hermione lived on in the house until they died. Hermione, who was a faithful member of the congregation at All Saints Church, died in 1994 and in her will left the house in Southfields as a place of learning and retreat. Beatrice Warren's only son died in 1958 when he was the vicar at St Mary and St Laurence church at Cauldon.

Christina Winterbottom

1861 – 1934

Christina Winterbottom was born in Stone in 1861, where she lived in Church Street with her older sister Amanda and her mother, Sarah Ann. The family lived with George and Hannah Bartlett who were Christina's uncle and aunt. George Bartlett was a cutler and grinder and Hannah a hawker, these are traditional gypsy occupations. Indeed Amanda and Christina were not the sister's given names Amanda was christened as Arminda in 1858 in Burnley and a will reveals that Christina's given name was Christiana. Sarah Ann Winterbottom, the girls mother, was the sister of Hannah Bartlett. The Winterbottom sisters stayed in Stone, living with their aunt and uncle, after their mother left to live in Oldham.

By 1881 Christina was an embroiderer who taught at the Leek Embroidery School. She stitched the panel of angels which is now part of Staffordshire Moorlands District Council's archive and which was recently featured in the BBC's *'The History of the World in a 100 objects'*.

Christina and her sister ran a fancy embroidery repository at 59 High Street in Stone. The business is advertised as a 'Church Embroidery Depot' in *Kelly's Post Office Directory* in 1904 and is the only church embroidery depot advertised in Staffordshire at that time. Christina left Stone between 1904 and 1911 and moved to Yorkshire where she was in business in Bilton at 8 Crab Lane as an Art Needlework dealer with two young women who also hailed from Staffordshire. Amanda Winterbottom stayed in Stone where she continued to run the Church Embroidery Depot for several years. She died in Stone in 1948. Christina died in Harrogate in 1934 leaving an estate of nearly £3,000.

Above
59 High Street, Stone, where the sisters ran a fancy embroidery repository

Right
A panel of angels stitched by Christina Winterbottom.

Staffordshire Moorlands District Council archives

‡ denotes one of Elizabeth Wardle's embroidery pupils

Allen, Alice
i. Facsimile of the Bayeux Tapestry
ii. Khartoum Altar frontal

Allen, Eliza
i. Traced cartoons of the replica of the Bayeux Tapestry borrowed from South Kensington Museum
ii. Designed the phoenix on white altar frontal at St Edward's church

Bate, Emily
i. Facsimile of the Bayeux Tapestry

Bentley, Emma Jane
i. Facsimile of the Bayeux Tapestry

Bill, Clara (nee Troost)
i. Stitched together panels of the Facsimile of the Bayeux Tapestry
ii. Khartoum Altar Frontal
iii. Restored the Edmund Street Altar frontal at St Edward's, Cheddleton.
iv. Madonna and Child panel at St Edward's, Cheddleton
v. Figures on a banner at St Peter's, Stoke

Bishop, Mary Ann (later Hunt)‡
i. Facsimile of the Bayeux Tapestry
ii. Four Kings Altar Frontal at St Edward's Church, Leek
iii. Agnus Dei and Rose alter frontal at St Luke's church with matching pulpit and lectern falls, bookmarkers and alms bags
iv. Fire screen once displayed in the office at Joshua Wardle's Leekbrook
v. May have stitched superfrontals for St Anne's church at Millersdale (no documentary evidence)

‡ denotes one of Elizabeth Wardle's embroidery pupils

Brunt, Annie Louise‡
i. Four Kings Altar Frontal at St Edward's Church, Leek

Cartwright, Ann‡
i. Facsimile of the Bayeux Tapestry
ii. Four Kings Altar Frontal at St Edward's Church, Leek

Challinor, Elizabeth
i. Khartoum Altar Frontal

Challinor, Kathleen
i. Khartoum Altar Frontal

Challinor, Jessie Mabel (later Phipps)
i. Facsimile of the Bayeux Tapestry
ii. Khartoum Altar Frontal

Challinor, Helen (Nellie)
i. Khartoum Altar Frontal

Challinor Mrs WE (Catherine)
i. Khartoum Altar Frontal

Mrs Edward Challinor (Janie)
i. Khartoum Altar Frontal

Clowes, Ann
i. Pelican frontal at St Luke's church, Leek
ii. Facsimile of the Bayeux Tapestry

Cruso, Ann
i. Handkerchief bag presented to Princess of Wales in 1881

‡ denotes one of Elizabeth Wardle's embroidery pupils

Dilworth, Ellen
i. Green lectern fall at All Saints, Leek
ii. Purple frontal and super frontal at All Saints designed by Tom Wardle

Eaton, Elizabeth
i. Facsimile of the Bayeux Tapestry

Ellis, Florence
i. Khartoum Altar Frontal

Fearon, Kathleen
i. Khartoum Altar Frontal

Fearon, Mary
i. Khartoum Altar Frontal

Fowler, Miss
i. Khartoum Altar Frontal

Frost, Elizabeth
i. Facsimile of the Bayeux Tapestry

Gailey, Frances (nee Ward)
i. Khartoum Altar Frontal

Garside, Mary Alice‡
i. Facsimile of the Bayeux Tapestry
ii. Four Kings Altar Frontal at St Edward's Church, Leek

Gater, Patience
i. Facsimile of the Bayeux Tapestry

Gillett, Mary Henrietta
i. Facsimile of the Bayeux Tapestry

‡ denotes one of Elizabeth Wardle's embroidery pupils

Gwynne, Mary Adeline
i. Facsimile of the Bayeux Tapestry

Hall, Kate
i. Khartoum Altar Frontal

Haynes, Elizabeth
i. Facsimile of the Bayeux Tapestry

Illiffe, Sarah
i. Facsimile of the Bayeux Tapestry

Lavington, Beatrice
i. Facsimile of the Bayeux Tapestry

Lowe, Anne Mills
i. Facsimile of the Bayeux Tapestry

Lowe, Beatrice Ellen (Nellie)
i. Four Kings Altar Frontal at St Edward's Church, Leek
ii. Secretary of Leek Embroidery Society

Lunn, Elizabeth Valentine
i. Facsimile of the Bayeux Tapestry
ii. Taught at Leek School of Embroidery

Maude, Geraldine
i. White Altar Frontal St Edward's, Leek with Elizabeth Wardle

McDonough, Mary Ellen‡
i. White Altar Frontal, Feast of Christ the King, for St Mary's RC Church, Leek (now missing)

‡ denotes one of Elizabeth Wardle's embroidery pupils

Mckenzie, Eliza (Lizzie)
i. Facsimile of the Bayeux Tapestry

Needham, Sarah
i. Pelican frontal at St Luke's church, Leek

Nicholson, Marianne
i. Panel, Certoza design, (Staffordshire Moorlands District Council Archive)

Edith Maud Nicholson
i. Four Kings Altar Frontal at St Edward's Church, Leek

Rose Nicholson
i. Four Kings Altar Frontal at St Edward's Church, Leek

Parker, Emily
i. Facsimile of the Bayeux Tapestry

Pattison, Alice
i. Facsimile of the Bayeux Tapestry

Pattison, Florence
i. Facsimile of the Bayeux Tapestry

Pearson, Florence
i. Facsimile of the Bayeux Tapestry

Pidcock, Elizabeth
i. Pelican frontal at St Luke's church, Leek
ii. Khartoum Altar Frontal

Price, Sarah Katherine (Kitty)‡
i. Four Kings Altar Frontal at St Edward's Church, Leek

‡ denotes one of Elizabeth Wardle's embroidery pupils

Redfern, Annie‡
i. Khartoum Altar Frontal
ii. Adjanta panel (Staffordshire Moorland District Council Archive)

Redfern, Frances Christina (Cissie)‡
i. Four Kings Altar Frontal at St Edward's Church, Leek

Ritchie, Margaret
i. Facsimile of the Bayeux Tapestry

Robinson, Charlotte
i. Four Kings Altar Frontal at St Edward's Church, Leek

Rowley, Anna Maria‡

Shute, Fanny
i. Pelican frontal at St Luke's church, Leek

Smith, Jennie
i. Facsimile of the Bayeux Tapestry

Smith, Ann
i. Facsimile of the Bayeux Tapestry
ii. Alter frontals at St Luke's church, Endon

Sutton, Ann
i. Pelican frontal at St Luke's church, Leek

Sutton, Mary Ellen
i. Pelican frontal at St Luke's church, Leek

Turnock, Mary
i. Facsimile of the Bayeux Tapestry
ii. Khartoum Altar Frontal

‡ denotes one of Elizabeth Wardle's embroidery pupils

Unwin, Constance
i. Khartoum Altar Frontal

Vigrass, Ellen (Nellie)‡
i. Four Kings Altar Frontal at St Edward's Church, Leek

Vigrass, Ethel
i. Framed panel at St Edward's church Leek

Ward, Mabel
i. Khartoum Altar Frontal

Warren, Beatrice Ethel
i. Altar frontals at St Chad's church, Longsdon
ii. Altar frontal at All Saints church, Hanley
iii. Altar frontal for Zanzibar Cathedral
iv. Chasuble for Holy Trinity, Hadley, Shropshire
v. Dorsal for Yarlet Hall school chapel
vi. Panel in All Saints church, Leek

Wardle, Ada
i. Khartoum Altar Frontal

Wardle, Ann (nee Welch)
i. Khartoum Altar Frontal

Wardle, Edith
i. Facsimile of the Bayeux Tapestry

Elizabeth Wardle
i. Pelican frontal at St Luke's church, Leek
ii. Facsimile of the Bayeux Tapestry
iii. Altar Frontals, Cheddleton, Ipstones, Leek, Meerbrook, Warslow etc

‡ denotes one of Elizabeth Wardle's embroidery pupils

Wardle, Elizabeth Leeke

i. Facsimile of the Bayeux Tapestry (few stitches)

Wardle, Ellinor

i. Khartoum Altar Frontal

Wardle, Grace

i. Khartoum Altar Frontal

Wardle, Lucy (nee Pidcock)

i. Khartoum Altar Frontal

Wardle, Lydia

i. Four Kings Altar Frontal at St Edward's Church, Leek
ii. Khartoum Altar Frontal
iii. Red Litany fall at All Saints, Leek
iv. Faces on a banner at St Peter's church, Stoke

Wardle, Margaret (later Worthington and Gaunt)

i. Facsimile of the Bayeux Tapestry
ii. Four Kings Altar Frontal at St Edward's Church, Leek
iii. Litany Fall (blue velvet) at All Saints, Leek
iv. White Cope, set of white chausible, maniple and stole designed by her brother Tom Wardle at All Saints, Leek

Wardle, Mildred

i. Khartoum Altar Frontal

Wardle, Phoebe

i. Facsimile of the Bayeux Tapestry
ii. Four Kings Altar Frontal at St Edward's Church, Leek

Watson, Margaret Eliza

i. Facsimile of the Bayeux Tapestry

‡ denotes one of Elizabeth Wardle's embroidery pupils

Watson, Mary Edith (nee Challinor)
i. Facsimile of the Bayeux Tapestry

Watson, Muriel
i. Khartoum Altar Frontal

Whittles, Catherine
i. Pelican frontal at St Luke's church, Leek

Winterbottom, Christina
i. Panel of Angels (Staffordshire Moorlands District Council Collection)
ii. Taught at Leek School of Embroidery

Worthington, Alice
i. Pelican frontal at St Luke's church, Leek

Worthington, Margaret Maud
i. Facsimile of the Bayeux Tapestry

Worthington, Rose
i. Pelican frontal at St Luke's church, Leek

Young, Mary
i. Pelican frontal at St Luke's church, Leek

Young, Sarah
i. Khartoum Altar Frontal
ii. Four Kings Altar Frontal at St Edward's Church, Leek
iii. Litany Fall, white cross on damask, at All Saints, Leek

Wardle Connection

Bold indicates women who stitched for Leek Embroidery Society

Many of the women who stitched for the Leek Embroidery Society were related to either **Elizabeth Wardle** or Thomas Wardle.

Daughters
Lydia, **Margaret**, **Edith** and **Elizabeth**.

Daughters-in-law
Lucy Pidcock was the wife of son Arthur. Lucy's mother was also a member of the society.

Ann Barnes Welch was the wife of son, Bernard.

Nieces
Eleanor, **Mildred**, **Grace** and **Ada Wardle** were the daughters of Thomas Wardle's brother, George.

Sisters-in-Law
Frances Wardle was the wife of George Wardle who was Thomas Wardle's brother.

Phoebe Wardle, Thomas Wardle's sister

Bold indicates women who stitched for Leek Embroidery Society

Cousins

Mary and **Sarah Young** were the daughters of Elizabeth Wardle's uncle, Samuel Young.

Others

Helen Dilworth was Elizabeth's first cousin once removed.

Mary Ann Bishop was Thomas Wardle's cousin once removed.

Samuel Young who was Elizabeth's uncle married Catherine Smith.

Catherine's sisters **Mary** and **Ann Smith** also stitched Leek Embroidery.

Catherine's sister, Margaret married Thomas Pattinson. Their daughters **Alice** and **Florence** stitched panels of the facsimile of the Bayeux Tapestry.

Alice and Florence Pattinson's cousin was Charles Philip Smith whose wife, **Jennie**, also worked on the facsimile of the Bayeux Tapestry.

Challinor Connections

Bold indicates women who stitched for Leek Embroidery Society

Mary Edith Watson (nee Challinor) was William Edward Challinor's sister and the cousin of **Jessie Mabel Phipps** (nee Challinor) and **Helen (Nellie) Challinor** who were the daughters of Joseph Challinor, a solicitor.

Mary Edith was the sister-in-law of **Margaret Watson** (nee Russell).

Catherine Challinor (nee Allen) was the wife of William Edward Challinor (Joseph's nephew), their daughters were **Kathleen** and **Elizabeth Challinor**.

Alice Allen was Catherine's sister.

Janie Challinor (nee Ellis) was the wife of Edward Challinor, a member of the Challinor family of solicitors.

Florence Bertha Ellis was Janie's niece who married William Francis Challinor, the son of William Edward Challinor and Catherine Allen.

Convoluted Connections

Bold indicates women who stitched for Leek Embroidery Society

Emma Jane Bentley's brother, John Joseph, was married to Ellen Grace. Ellen was the sister of Thomas Grace who married **Ann Walker**.

Mary Adeline Gwynne (nee Jones) was the sister of Eveline Jones who married George H Hall. George Hall was the brother of **Kate Hall**. **Mary Gwynne** and Katie Hall were sisters-in-law.

Mabel Ward was the niece of **Frances Ward** who married John Gailey

Christina Redfern and **Annie Redfern** were cousins.

The Wardle Family Tree

Joshua Wardle

Mary Darlington

- Thomas Wardle
  1831-1909

  Elizabeth Wardle
  1834-1902

- Elizabeth Wardle
  1833-1912

  John Illsley

- George Wardle
  1835-1912

  Frances Martha Bray

- **Ann Wardle**
  1837 -1927

- **Martha Phoebe Wardle**
  1839 - 1890

Bold indicates women who stitched for Leek Embroidery Society

*George Wardle is Thomas Wardle's brother and his children are cousins to Thomas Wardle's children

There is no evidence that Thomas and Elizabeth Wardle are distantly related even though they share the same surname.

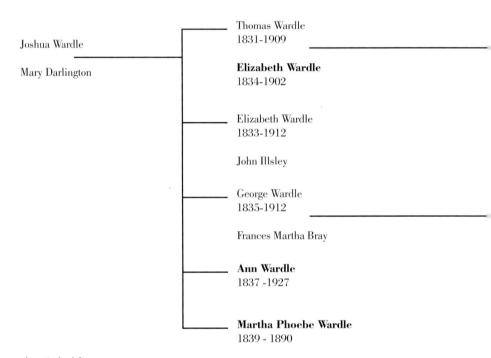

Gilbert Charles Wardle
1862-1943

(1) Mary Challinor
(2) **Katharine Fearon**

Arthur Henry Wardle
1863-1916

Lucy Pidcock

Bernard Wardle
1865-1931

Ann Welch

Frederick Wardle
1866-1958

Mary Poppleton

Lydia Y Wardle
1868-1949

Margaret Wardle
1869-1949

(1) Philip Worthington
(2) Guy Gaunt

Tom Wardle
1871-1925

Gabrielle Gueret

Edith Wardle
1872-1925

Walter Underhill

Elizabeth Leeke Wardle†
1877-1946

Horace Wardle*
(her cousin)

Eleanor Wardle
1865-1947

Mildred Wardle
1867-1958

Horace Wardle
1869 -1933

Elizabeth Leeke Wardle†*
(his cousin)

Grace Wardle
1871 - 1954

John Illsley (her cousin)

Ada Wardle
1873-1956

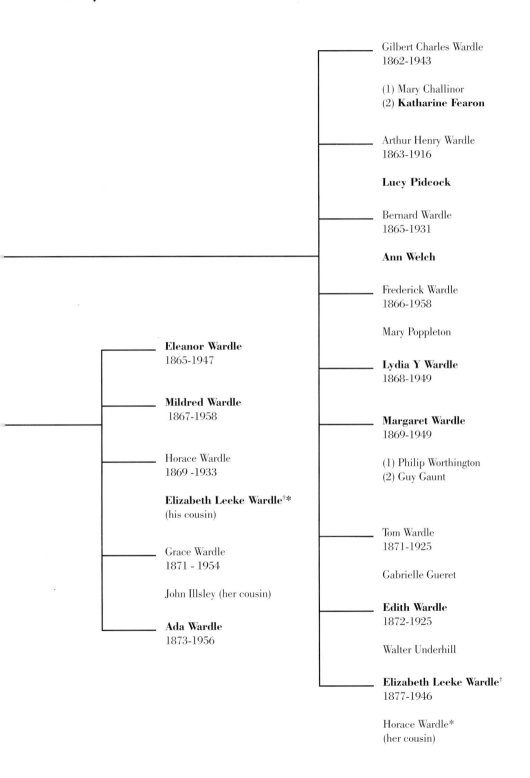

The Young Family Tree

- Samuel Young 1770 -1833
  Thomasina Leeke 1774 - 1823
  - Elizabeth Young 1802 -1871
    Hugh Wardle
  - Barnet Young
  - Samuel Young 1806 - 1885
    Catherine Smith* 1812 - 1860
  - Lydia Young
  - William Young
  - George Young
  - Mary T Young
  - Charles Young
  - John Young

Bold indicates women who stitched for Leek Embroidery Society

*Catherine Smith had several siblings;
Her sister Ann (1822- 1901) stitched Leek Embroidery.
Her sister Margaret (1827– 1898) married Thomas Pattinson.
Her daughters Alice Pattinson (1864 -1936) and Florence Pattinson (1866 -1940) stitched part of the Replica of the Bayeux Tapestry.

Elizabeth Wardle
1834-1902

Thomas Wardle

Catherine Young
1836 - 1881

Robert Bennison

Helen Bennison

Frederick Dilworth

Barnett Young

Sarah Young
1848 -1933

Mary Young
1850 - 1921

Thomas Hulme

Annie

The Challinor Family Tree

- William Challinor
  Mary Shelmerdine
  - William Challinor
    1821 - 1896
    Elizabeth Pemberton
  - Mary Challinor
  - Edward Challinor
  - John Challinor
  - Joseph Challinor
    1828 - 1910
    Jessie Woodcroft
  - Charles Challinor

Bold indicates women who stitched for
Leek Embroidery Society

William Edward Challinor
1852 - 1896

Catherine Allen
1856 - 1950

Mary K Challinor
1854 - 1857

Mary Edith Challinor
1858 - 1898

Charles Watson

Edward Challinor
1862 - 1906

Janie R C Ellis

Jessica Mabel Challinor
1864 - 1926

Constantine O Phipps

Mary B Challinor
1865 - 1901

Gilbert Wardle

Helen Challinor
1867 - 1938

Jessie Challinor
1868

Albert Muntz

Percy Challinor
1874

Hilda Challinor
1875

John Evershed

Kathleen Mary Challinor
1880 - 1977

John Ward
1879 - 1875

William Francis Challinor
1882

Florence Ellis
1887 - 1924

Elizabeth Challinor
1883 - 1922

Arthur Gaunt

John Challinor

Mary Atkins

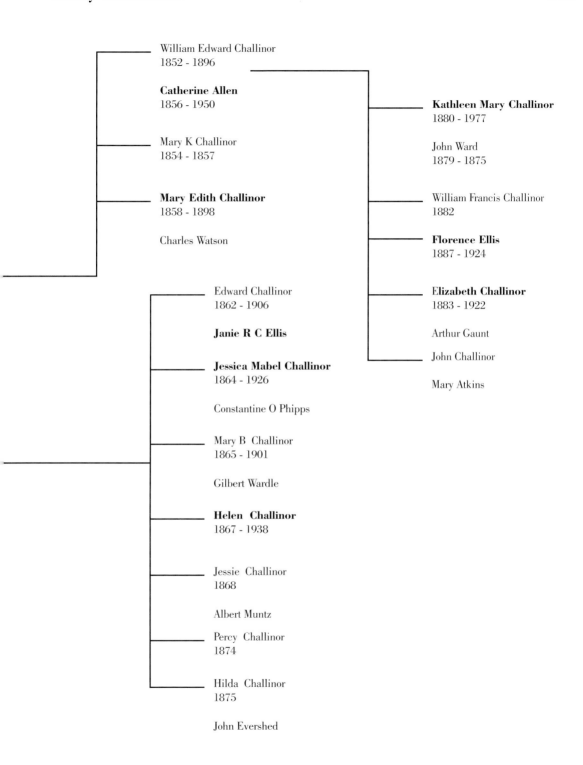

Sources

Civil Registration records of Births, Marriages and Deaths

Parish Registers of Christenings, Marriages and Burials

Census Returns, 1841 to 1911

Probate Records

Leek Library Local Studies Archive
- Boxes of material relating to Leek Embroidery Society, Bayeux Tapestry, Elizabeth Wardle and Leek Embroidery Society
- Leek Annuals
- Mens Time Book – Ledger of hours worked (1845-1853) Joshua Wardle Ltd
- Minutes of Leek Charity Organization Society
- Minutes of Leek Amateur Musical Society
- Photographic Archive
- The Johnson Collection

Newspapers

Bucks Herald

Derby Mercury

Exeter and Plymouth Gazette

Hull Daily Mail

Leek Post

Leek Post and Times

Leek Times

Lichfield

London Gazette

Manchester Courier and Lancashire General Advertiser

Manchester Evening News

Norfolk Chronicle

Pall Mall Gazette

Staffordshire Advertiser

Staffordshire Sentinel

Tamworth Herald

Books

Cleverdon, Faith, 'Church Parish and People', Delmar Press Ltd, 2012

Crichton-Harris, Ann, 'Poison in Small Measure: Dr Christopherson and the Cure for Bilharzia', Brill Academic Publishers, 2009

Crisp, William, 'Some Account of the Diocese of Bloemfontein in the Province of South Africa from 1863 to 1894', 1895

Ferguson, Robert, 'The Short Sharp Life of T.E. Hulme', faber & faber, 2002

Fisher, Michael, 'A Soldier's India', Caron Publications, 1986.

Greenslade, M W, 'A History of the County of Stafford: Volume VII: Leek and the Moorlands', Victoria County History, 1996

Horsefield, Thomas Walker, 'The History, Antiquities and Topography of the County of Sussex', Sussex Press, 1835

Inder, Pam & Aldis, Marion, 'Susanna's Carpet', Deepings Court Publications, 1998

Jacques, Anne, 'Leek Embroidery', 1990

Jacques, Anne, 'The Wardle Story', Churnet Valley Books, 1996

Johnson, Beryl, 'Old St Edward Street', 1993

King, Brenda M, 'Dye, Print, Stitch', 2009

'Leek Trade Bills c. 1830-1930', Vol 1, Churnet Valley Books, 2003

'Leek Trade Bills c. 1830-1930, Vol 3, Churnet Valley Books, 2003

Lewis, C & Edwards, G.E., 'Historical Records of the Church of the Province of South Africa', SPCK, 1934

Milner, Robert, 'Cheddleton, a village history', Moorland Co. Ltd, 1983

Milner, Robert, 'Cheddleton 1841', Churnet Valley Books, 2012

Oxford Dictionary of National Biography

Poole, Ray, 'A History of Leek', Churnet Valley Books, 2002

Poole, Ray, 'Leek's Golden Years', Churnet Valley Books', 2009

Sims. Rupert, 'Bibliotheca Staffordiensis', A.C. Lomax,1853

Stuart, D. G., 'The History of the Leek Embroidery Society', University of Keele, 1969

Walton, Cathryn & Porter, Lindsey, 'Spirit of Leek : 1', Landmark Publishing, 2000

Walton, Cathryn & Porter, Lindsey, 'Spirit of Leek : 2', Landmark Publishing, 2001

Walton, Cathryn & Porter, Lindsey, 'Spirit of Leek : 3' The Textile Mills, Landmark Publishing, 2002

Walton, Cathryn, 'Spirit of Leek : 4', Landmark Publishing, 2005

Walton, Cathryn & Porter, Lindsey, 'Lost Houses of North Staffordshire', Landmark Publishing, 2006

Wirgman, A. Theodore, 'Storm and Sunshine in South Africa', Longmans, 1922

Directories

Kelly's Directory of the Counties of Derby, Notts, Leicester and Rutland, London, (May, 1891) - p.204-205

Kelly's Directories of Staffordshire

Kelly's Directories of Shropshire

Morris, J.S.C, 'Business Directory of London', 1884

Tillotsons Directory for Westhoughton 1896 - 1898

Magazines

St Luke's Parish Magazine, 1873

St Edward's Parish magazine, 1895

Websites

http://www.ancestry.com

https://familysearch.org

http:///www.findmypast.co.uk

http://staffordshirebmd.org.uk/

http://www.ukwhoswho.com

http://www.bednallarchive
A database of original documents in the Bednall Collection which provide information on the silk industry of Leek and other aspects of local history.

https://www.dur.ac.uk
GB-0033-SAD Khartoum Cathedral, material relating to service in the Sudan

http://www.ucl.ac.uk/bloomsbury-project/articles/events/conference2008/mitchell.pdf
Mitchell, Charlotte. Women students at UCL in the early 1880s

Photographs

Photographs of ecclesiastical embroideries in St Edward's Church Leek by kind permission of Richard Kniseley-Marpole.

The author acknowledges that a number of the photographs used in this publication are reproduced with the permission of the Staffordshire County Council and others with the permission of Staffordshire Moorlands District Council.

Several photographs used in this publication are from the photographic archive of Leek and District Historical Society.

Additional photography by Cathryn Walton

Acknowledgements

The author wishes to thank everyone who has helped with proof reading, photographs, recollections and advice.

John and Catherine Braddock
Janet Bray
George Walton

Anne Addison, David Ball, Jane Baxter, Alan Bednall, Judith Billing, Nigel Brealey, Brendon Carr at Reading Museum, Faith Cleverdon, Joan Cooper, Stella Done, Michael Fisher, Christine Green, Peter Hall, Sheila Hine, John and Jean Hunt, Henry and Christina Jebb, Maria Killoran, Louise Kirtley, Brenda King, Pat Lamb, Shirley Machin, Robert Milner, John Newall, Suzanne Shallcross, Linda Skellam, Peter Stretch, Adrian and Jacquie Sumerling, Chris Thompson, Carol Victor, Africana Librarian, Main Library, Nelson Mandela Bay Municipality, Port Elizabeth, John and Gill White.

And anyone else inadvertently omitted

Brenda King has researched the work of the Leek Embroidery society for more than 20 years. Her most recent publication 'Stitch and Stone: A History of the Leek Embroidery Society' will be published in 2015.